THE WORLD WARS

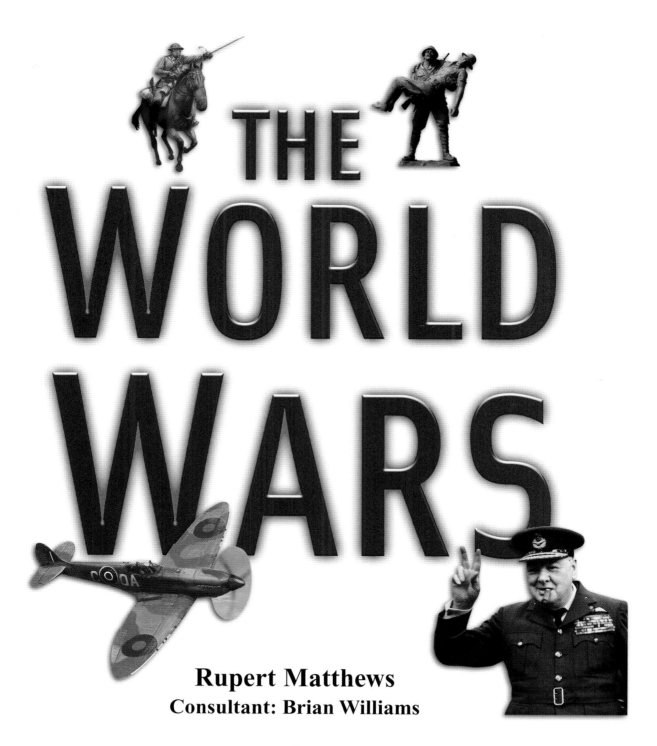

THE WORLD WARS

Rupert Matthews
Consultant: Brian Williams

BARDFIELD
PRESS

Editorial Director: Art Director:
Belinda Gallagher   Jo Brewer

Editor: Designer:
Amanda Askew   Stephan Davis

Cover Designer: Indexer:
Tony Collins   Jane Parker

Reprographics: Production Manager:
Stephan Davis, Liberty Newton   Elizabeth Brunwin

First published in 2007 by Bardfield Press
Copyright © Miles Kelly Publishing Ltd 2007

Bardfield Press is an imprint of
Miles Kelly Publishing Ltd
Bardfield Centre, Great Bardfield, Essex, CM7 4SL

10 9 8 7 6 5 4 3 2 1

ISBN 978-1-84236-809-1

Printed in China

British Library Cataloguing-in-Publication Data
A catalogue record for this book is available from the British Library

ACKNOWLEDGEMENTS
All artworks are from the Miles Kelly Artwork Bank

All photographs are from Corel, ILN, PhotoDisc

www.mileskelly.net
info@mileskelly.net

CONTENTS

WORLD WAR I

1914–1918

Caporetto
Marne
Gallipoli
Somme
Verdun
Jutland
League of
Nations
Allies
Tannenberg
Ypres

1914

When Europe goes to war, many believe that it will be a short conflict, with fighting over by Christmas.

AUSTRIA–HUNGARY ATTACKS SERBIA – WAR BEGINS

🤝 25. Kaiser Wilhelm II of Germany informs France and Britain that he will mobilize the entire German armed forces unless Russia agrees to cease its partial mobilization within three days.

🤝 30. The Netherlands declares that it will remain neutral in any war resulting from the murder of Archduke Franz Ferdinand.

🤝 31. Germany asks France to explain what its position would be if war were to break out between Germany and Russia.

▶ The German ruler, Kaiser Wilhelm II, wanted Germany to gain the power and prestige that he believed it was entitled to.

🤝 23. Austria–Hungary delivers an ultimatum to Serbia following the murder in June of Austrian Archduke Franz Ferdinand by a Serb. If accepted, Austria–Hungary would control Serbia.

🤝 25. Serbia accepts nine of the ten terms of the ultimatum. Austria–Hungary refuses.

🤝 25. Tzar Nicholas II of Russia orders a partial mobilization. Russian troops march towards Serbia to defend against the Austro-Hungarian invasion.

🤝 28. Austria–Hungary declares war on Serbia.

🤝 29. Bulgaria declares itself neutral in the dispute between Serbia and Austria–Hungary.

☀ 30. The first shots of the war are fired when Austro-Hungarian warships on the river Danube open fire on the Serbian capital of Belgrade.

🤝 30. Germany warns Russia to demobilize its army or risk war.

◀ Archduke Franz Ferdinand and his wife prepare to climb into their car just minutes before they were both shot dead.

🤝 25. Italy, a partner with Germany and Austria–Hungary in the Triple Alliance, does not join with Germany in diplomatic moves to put pressure on Russia.

♠ 28. British First Lord of the Admiralty, Winston Churchill, orders the Royal Navy to steam to prearranged war stations, and to prepare for action.

♠ 29. The German High Seas Fleet is ordered to take up battle stations.

RETREAT FROM MONS

WESTERN FRONT

🤝 1. Belgium declares that it will remain neutral.

🤝 1. France orders a general mobilization.

⚔ 2. Germany invades neutral Luxembourg.

🤝 2. Germany asks Belgium for permission to use Belgian roads. Belgium refuses.

🤝 2. Germany declares war on France.

🤝 4. Germany declares war on Belgium.

⚔ 4. German armies invade Belgium.

🤝 4. Britain demands that German armies retreat from Belgium. No reply is received, so Britain declares war on Germany.

⚔ 8. Battle of Mulhouse. French armies invade Germany.

🤝 10. France declares war on Austria–Hungary. Britain follows.

⚔ 18. Belgian army retreats to Antwerp.

⚔ 23. British forces at Mons in Belgium are attacked by German forces.

⚔ 25. French invasion of Germany halted.

⚔ 25. Retreat from Mons. British forces fall back into France.

⚔ 25. Battle of the Marne begins.

EASTERN FRONT

🤝 1. Germany declares war on Russia.

🤝 3. Romania declares that it will remain neutral.

🤝 5. Austria–Hungary declares war on Russia.

🤝 5. Montenegro declares war on Austria–Hungary.

🤝 5. Serbia declares war on Germany.

⚔ 12. Battle of river Jadar. Austro-Hungarian armies invade Serbia.

⚔ 20. Russian armies invade Germany near Gumbinnen. Kaiser Wilhelm II appoints General Paul von Hindenburg to command the defence, assisted by General Erich Ludendorff.

⚔ 21. Battle of river Jadar. Serbian forces halt the Austro-Hungarian armies.

⚔ 23. Battle of Krasnik. Austria–Hungary invades Russia.

⚔ 23. Battle of Tannenberg. German armies crush the Russian 2nd Army, inflicting massive losses and halting the Russian invasion of Germany.

THE MED AND MIDDLE EAST

♣ 2. Germany signs a secret treaty with Turkey. Under the treaty, Germany promises to aid Turkey if war should break out with Russia. Turkey promises to shelter German warships.

🤝 3. Italy declares that it will remain neutral in the war despite the Triple Alliance.

⚔ 4. German warships *Breslau* and *Goeben* open fire on the ports of Bône and Philippeville in French Algeria.

🤝 10. German warships *Breslau* and *Goeben* take refuge in Turkish waters.

REST OF THE WORLD

⚓ 6. German cruiser *Königsberg* sinks British cruiser *Pegasus* off Mombasa in East Africa.

🤝 15. Japan demands that Germany hand over the port of Tsingtao on the Chinese coast.

🤝 15. Japan later declares war on Germany.

⚔ 20. British troops from Nigeria invade German Cameroons and later capture German Togoland.

KEY   🤝 DIPLOMACY   🏠 HOME   ⚓ NAVAL   ♣ SECRET WAR   ⚔ BATTLE

BATTLE OF THE MARNE

⚜ 4. Battle of the Marne. British and French armies begin to counter attack Germans along the river Marne.

⚜ 7. Battle of the Marne. German counter attack is halted when French General Joseph Gallieni rushes reinforcements to the front from Paris in taxi cabs.

⚜ 9. Battle of the Marne. British forces cross the river Marne to push deep into German lines near Chateau Thierry. Belgian armies attack the Germans near Antwerp.

⚜ 9. Battle of the Aisne. British and French forces halt as the German retreat stops on the river Aisne.

⚜ 17. British aircraft bomb German airship bases at Cologne and Düsseldorf.

⚜ 22. Race to the Sea. British and French armies seek to outflank German armies in Picardy. The Germans respond by marching north towards Péronne.

⚜ 27. Race to the Sea. German armies attack at Artois in an attempt to outflank the British. French armies march up to block the move.

⚜ 3. Battle of Rava Ruska. Austro-Hungarian invasion of Russia ceases and is thrown back with a loss of 350,000 men.

⚜ 11. Battle of Rava Ruska. Austro-Hungarian forces retreat, evacuating Lemberg.

⚜ 11. Battle of the river Drina. Austro-Hungarian forces invade Serbia and march towards Belgrade.

⚑ 17. The Germans learn of Russian plans to invade the key coal-mining area of Silesia. German troops are rushed south by rail.

⚜ 28. Battle of the Vistula. German armies led by Hindenburg attack Russian armies along the river Vistula. Although outnumbered by three to one, the Germans advance steadily. Russia calls off plans for the invasion of Silesia.

⚜ 30. Battle of the Vistula. Hindenburg calls off the German attack.

🤝 17. Australia pledges to support Britain 'to the last man and the last shilling'.

⚓ 22. German U-boat U-9 sinks three British cruisers in about 30 minutes off the Dutch coast.

WAR SPREADS AROUND THE WORLD

WESTERN FRONT

☀ 6. Siege of Antwerp. Belgian forces begin to evacuate the city.

☀ 10. Siege of Antwerp. The remaining Belgian forces in the city surrender to the Germans.

⬥ 13. The first Canadian troops land in Plymouth, England. They will later be moved to France to fight on the Western Front.

☀ 18. Battle of the Yser. Sir John French orders his British forces to attack across the river Yser towards Lille and Menin. The move is designed to protect the key transport centre of Ypres.

⬥ 19. King Albert of Belgium orders the sea defences to be breached, flooding large areas of northern Belgium in an attempt to halt the German advance towards Nieuport.

☀ 29. First Battle of Ypres. German commander in chief Erich von Falkenhayn launches a major assault on the Belgian city of Ypres, held by the British.

☀ 31. First Battle of Ypres. British troops stop the German attack at Gheluvelt.

EASTERN FRONT

☀ 3. Austro-Hungarian armies advance from Galicia to support Hindenburg's right wing.

☀ 9. Massive Russian reinforcements begin to arrive on the river Vistula.

☀ 17. Hindenburg orders the German and Austro-Hungarian armies to retreat from the river Vistula before the expected Russian attack takes place. The retreating troops are ordered to steal all food and burn all buildings as they retreat so as to hinder the Russian advance.

▼ The German submarines, known as U-boats, proved to be one of the most effective new weapons to be used in World War I.

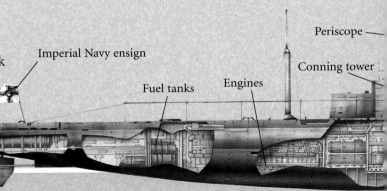

Periscope

Imperial Navy ensign

Conning tower

Fuel tanks   Engines

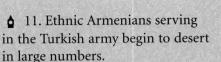

Propeller

THE MED AND MIDDLE EAST

⬥ 11. Ethnic Armenians serving in the Turkish army begin to desert in large numbers.

🖐 17. Turkish secret service agents report that weapons are being smuggled over the border from Russia to arm Armenian rebels.

☀ 23. Units of the British–Indian army invade Mesopotamia, part of the Turkish Empire to protect British oil supplies.

REST OF THE WORLD

⬥ 16. The first New Zealand troops leave Wellington to steam to Britain for war service.

⬥ 20. The first Australian troops leave Sydney to steam to Britain.

⚓ 20. German U-boat U-17 sinks British cargo ship *Glitra* off the Norwegian coast. This is the first merchant ship ever to be sunk by a submarine.

FIRST YPRES

BATTLE OF THE FALKLANDS

3. First Battle of Ypres. The Germans renew their attack and capture Dixmunde, north of Ypres.

3. German warships attack British east coast towns.

8. British intelligence establishes 'Room 40', an organization that cracks the codes of German military radio signals.

12. First Battle of Ypres. Heavy snows bring an end to the German attack.

15. Battle of Champagne. Joint British and French attack fails to achieve much success against the newly constructed German trenches.

25. Christmas Truce. At several sections of the Western Front an unofficial truce takes place. Fighting ceases as soldiers sing carols, swap presents and cook festive meals. German and British regiments organize international football matches. In most places the truce ends on Boxing Day.

5. Battle of Belgrade. Renewed Austro-Hungarian assault on the Serb capital begins. Belgrade is captured after three weeks.

11. Battle of Lodz. An offensive by German 9th Army led by General von Mackensen is halted. A Russian counter attack surrounds the German attack forces. The battle ends on 25 November.

9. Battle of Belgrade. Serb forces recapture Belgrade and drive Austro-Hungarian armies out of Serbia. The fighting for Belgrade has cost the Austro-Hungarians 230,000 killed, wounded or captured, and the Serbs 170,000 – almost half their army.

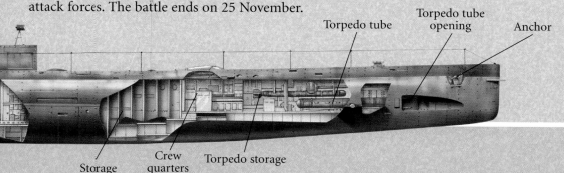

Torpedo tube

Torpedo tube opening

Anchor

Storage

Crew quarters

Torpedo storage

4. Battle of Qurna. British forces land from the sea and capture the Turkish town.

18. Britain declares it will take temporary control of Egypt and moves troops to the area.

1. Battle of Coronel. German Pacific Fleet sinks two British cruisers off Chile.

10. Japan captures German base of Tsingtao in China.

8. Battle of the Falklands. German Pacific Fleet is attacked by British South Atlantic Squadron. Only one of the five German ships escapes – the cruiser *Dresden*.

1915

As the war engulfs most of the world, men from many nations join the fighting.

POISON GAS

🤝 13. The British War Cabinet decides that priority must be given to forcing Turkey to reopen the Dardanelles. Since the sea lane was blocked, Russian exports have collapsed and it has become almost impossible for Britain or France to send weapons and supplies to Russia. First Lord of the Admiralty Winston Churchill is given the task of drawing up a plan.

🗲 19. German Zeppelin airships bomb several towns in England. British aircraft are unable to fly as high as the Zeppelins.

⚔ 13. Battle of Bolimov. Poison gas is used for the first time in warfare by the German 9th Army under General von Mackensen. Problems with the weather make the gas ineffective and the German attack towards Warsaw is halted with comparative ease by the Russians after four weeks of fighting.

🤝 20. Austria–Hungary is forced to withdraw troops from the Eastern Front to the Alps as relations with Italy become increasingly difficult.

⚔ 3. Battle of Sarikamish. A Turkish attack on Kars is defeated by the Russians. Turkish commander Enver Pasha resigns.

🤝 11. Greece refuses to join the Allies, despite being offered Turkish territory in return.

⚓ 24. Battle of Dogger Bank. British and German battle-cruiser fleets meet in the North Sea. The German battle-cruiser *Blücher* is sunk.

MASURIAN LAKES   SHELL SCANDAL

1. The German government starts to ration bread as Britain's naval blockade of German ports takes effect.

▼ British infantry attacking from their trenches went 'over the top' of the trench parapet to race forwards.

10. Battle of Neuve-Chappelle. British commander in France, Sir John French, begins a four-day attack to test new weapons and tactics.

27. The Shell Scandal. Sir John French announces that the British army is dangerously short of ammunition, particularly artillery shells. A major political row develops with national newspapers criticizing the government.

1. The Austro-Hungarian government starts to ration bread.

7. Battle of the Masurian Lakes. The Germans under Hindenburg in East Prussia drive back the Russians by 110 km and capture 90,000 prisoners.

7. Poor weather and supply systems halt an Austro-Hungarian attack on the Russians in Gallicia.

22. Siege of Przemysl. The key Austro-Hungarian strategic transport centre of Przemysl, which has been under siege for weeks, finally surrenders to the Russians.

3. Battle of Suez. Turkish assault on the Suez Canal is driven off by British troops in Egypt.

14. The Turkish government begins a murderous crackdown on Armenian rebels.

18. The British Mediterranean Fleet fails to force a passage through the Dardanelles, losing three ships. The British government orders Admiral de Robeck to make a second attempt using land forces as well as warships.

4. Germany announces that all merchant ships heading towards Britain will be sunk.

22. South Africa sends spies into the German colony of Southwest Africa.

18. South Africa invades German Southwest Africa (Namibia) with 21,000 troops led by General Louis Botha.

SECOND BATTLE OF YPRES – 'BLOODY WIPERS'

WESTERN FRONT

⚔ 10. Battle of St Mihiel. French attacks at St Mihiel near the Meuse begin well, but soon falter as German defences prove too strong.

🕵 19. German engineers invent an interrupter gear to allow machine guns to fire forwards through an aircraft propeller. This allows the Germans to develop an effective fighter aircraft and to dominate the skies.

⚔ 22. Second Battle of Ypres. German attack on the British at Ypres opens with a successful gas attack.

EASTERN FRONT

◄ *A British cavalryman and his horse charge forwards wearing anti-gas masks. The gas attack should have allowed the cavalry to break through the German lines and attack, but this failed to happen.*

THE MED AND MIDDLE EAST

🏠 Turkish troops begin a series of massacres of suspected rebels in Armenia.

⚔ 25. Gallipoli. The British–French landings at Gallipoli beside the Dardanelles begin, but poor organization leads to confusion.

REST OF THE WORLD

ATTACK AT GALLIPOLI CHANTILLY CONFERENCE

☀ 6. Second Battle of Ypres. British counter attacks fail to succeed. The area is given a new commander – General Herbert Plummer.

☀ 9. Battle of Artois. A French offensive begins with an advance of 6 km in two hours, but the key Vimy Ridge is not captured.

☀ 25. Second Battle of Ypres. German attacks end in failure, but the British front line is now only 5 km in front of Ypres.

⬥ 25. A new British coalition government is formed under Liberal Herbert Asquith.

⬥ 1. British government allows women to work in munitions factories for the first time.

🤝 1. Germany issues a formal apology to the USA for sinking an American merchant ship.

☀ 16. Battle of Artois. The French offensive climaxes with an assault by 20 divisions, but Vimy Ridge is still in German hands.

⬥ 24. Chantilly Conference. Senior British and French commanders in France meet to decide on future strategy. They decide to launch a major offensive in September.

☀ 1. The Germans begin a joint attack with the Austro-Hungarians in Galicia on a 45-km-wide front. After five days of fighting, the Russian 3rd Army collapses.

☀ 6. The Germans capture the city of Gorlice from the Russians.

▶ *An Australian war memorial commemorates the heroic spirit of the Australian troops at Gallipoli and the legendary 'mateship' shown towards each other by the fighting men.*

☀ 3. The joint German-Austro-Hungarian attack in Galicia continues with the recapture of the key fortress city of Przemysl.

☀ 22. The Austro-Hungarians recapture Lemburg in Galicia. The Hungarian city has been in Russian hands for nine months.

☀ 6. Gallipoli. The Turks halt the British attack.

☀ 19. Gallipoli. Australian and New Zealand Army Corps (ANZAC) halt a Turkish attack.

🤝 23. Italy declares war on Austria–Hungary over a border dispute in the Alps.

☀ 4. Gallipoli. Turkish forces halt a renewed ANZAC attack.

☀ 30. First Battle of Isonzo. Italians drive the Austro-Hungarians back to the river Isonzo, but fail to cross it.

⚓ 7. British liner *Lusitania* is sunk off Ireland by a German U-boat – 124 Americans are killed.

☀ 11. South African troops capture Windhoek in German Southwest Africa.

WARSAW ATTACKED

THE FOKKER SCOURGE

WESTERN FRONT

9. British secretary for war, Lord Kitchener, begins a major recruitment drive. Over 2 million men volunteer within three weeks.

▶ *Lord Kitchener was scornful of the idea of armoured fighting vehicles – tanks – but others were more enthusiastic.*

1. The Fokker Scourge. The German interrupter gear claims its first aircraft victim. Fokker aircraft gain superiority over British and French air forces.

4. The Germans arrest British nurse Edith Cavell on charges of espionage.

12. British engineers begin work on the armoured vehicle moving on tracks that will later become known as the tank.

EASTERN FRONT

13. Battle of Warsaw begins as the German 12th Army attacks from East Prussia.

17. Bulgaria signs a secret treaty with Germany promising to attack Russia. Germany promises to give Bulgaria parts of neighbouring countries if they win the war.

21. Russia's Tzar Nicholas II sacks his commander in chief and takes command of the Russian armed forces. He moves to the military command post, leaving domestic government to his wife and ministers.

25. Battle of Warsaw. German advance on Warsaw continues with the capture of the city of Brest-Litovsk.

28. Germany offers Russia peace. The Tzar refuses unless all German troops retreat.

THE MED AND MIDDLE EAST

18. Second Battle of Isonzo. A new Italian attack again fails to cross the river Isonzo.

24. Battle of Nasiriya. A British army marching through Mesopotamia towards Baghdad defeats Turkish resistance.

6. Gallipoli. New British landings at Suvla Bay attempt to break the deadlock, but fail due to poor organization.

20. Italy declares war on Turkey.

REST OF THE WORLD

9. German forces in Southwest Africa surrender to South Africa.

11. German cruiser *Königsberg* is destroyed off East Africa, but the crew escape.

26. After renewed US protests, Germany ends the practice of attacking merchant ships without warning.

▼ *A German pilot uses the forward-firing machine gun on his Fokker Eindecker to shoot down a British gun bus. The Fokker was so deadly that British pilots called it 'the Fokker Scourge'.*

BATTLE OF LOOS

EDITH CAVELL

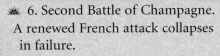

WESTERN FRONT

⚔ 25. Second Battle of Champagne begins. Major French attack breaks through German trenches, but reinforcements do not arrive in time to exploit the success.

⚔ 25. Third Battle of Artois begins. Major French attack again fails to capture Vimy Ridge.

⚔ 25. Battle of Loos begins. Major British attack fails to advance against strong German field fortifications.

⚔ 6. Second Battle of Champagne. A renewed French attack collapses in failure.

⚓ 7. The Germans execute British nurse Edith Cavell despite many international calls for mercy.

⚔ 13. Battle of Loos. A fresh British attack succeeds in capturing the German Hohenzollern Redoubt fortress.

◀ *Nurse Edith Cavell was executed by the Germans for helping British soldiers to escape capture.*

EASTERN FRONT

🤝 22. Bulgaria begins to mobilize its army.

⚔ 25. Battle of Warsaw. German advance reaches Vilna.

⚔ Battle of Warsaw. Heavy rains bring a halt to the German offensive.

⚔ 6. A new joint German and Austro-Hungarian invasion of Serbia begins.

🤝 14. Bulgaria declares war on Serbia and invades, attacking the Serb army from the rear.

🤝 15. France, Britain and Montenegro declare war on Bulgaria.

🤝 19. Italy and Russia declare war on Bulgaria.

THE MED AND MIDDLE EAST

⚔ 16. The British forces in Mesopotamia reach the key river town of Kut-el-Armana.

🤝 27. Greece agrees to allow the Allies to use the port of Salonika as a supply base.

⚔ 28. British forces capture Kut-el-Armana.

⚔ 18. Third Battle of Isonzo. Sudden heavy rains halt a new Italian attack.

REST OF THE WORLD

▶ *Equipped with a small gun and carrying only three men, this light tank could move quickly to attack enemy infantry, but was highly vulnerable to artillery fire.*

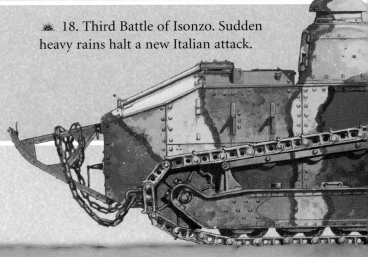

KEY 🤝 DIPLOMACY ⌂ HOME ⚓ NAVAL ⚔ SECRET WAR ⚔ BATTLE

SERB RETREAT

HAIG TAKES COMMAND

3. The government appoints General Joseph Joffre to command all French forces on the Western Front.

6. Second Chantilly Conference. Senior British and French commanders in France decide to launch a major offensive in the summer of 1916.

17. Sir John French is sacked as commander of British forces on the Western Front and replaced by Douglas Haig.

28. Britain introduces conscription of able-bodied men into the armed forces.

▲ The trenches were reinforced with timber supports to make them stronger.

5. Bulgarian forces capture Serb city of Nis, threatening the rear of the Serb army.

23. The Serb army abandons all attempts to defeat their enemies. The 71-year-old King Peter refuses to surrender and announces he will walk over the snow-capped mountains to neutral Albania. Most of his army decides to follow. Having destroyed all vehicles and artillery to stop them being captured, the Serbs disappear into the snow. Pursuing Bulgarian forces refuse to follow.

15. The Serb army begins to arrive in the Albanian town of Scutari, which they fortify. It is estimated that about one-third of the Serbs died on the march.

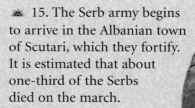

▶ A British soldier of 1915. He has puttees wrapped around his legs for protection against mud and a steel helmet to give protection from shell splinters.

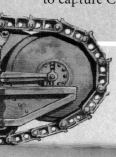

10. Fourth Battle of Isonzo begins. Another Italian attack fails to break Austro-Hungarian lines.

22. British forces in Mesopotamia fail to capture Ctesiphon and fall back to Kut.

7. British forces at Kut are surrounded.

8. Gallipoli. British and Anzac forces begin to evacuate their positions.

10. Fourth Battle of Isonzo ends. The city of Gorizia is totally destroyed.

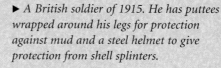

1916

Huge armies with modern weaponry face each other, leading to slaughter on a massive scale.

GALLIPOLI EVACUATED

19. The first trials take place of the British secret weapon codenamed 'Mother', later to be called the tank.

24. Newly appointed Admiral Reinhard Scheer, commander of the German navy, formulates a plan to ambush and destroy the British Grand Fleet in the North Sea.

27. General Erich von Falkenhayn, German senior commander, informs Kaiser Wilhelm II of plans to inflict massive casualties on the French with a strategy of controlled attrition at the fortress city of Verdun.

4. Top secret Austro-Hungarian government report states that the Allies will win the war.

5. Austro-Hungarians invade Montenegro. The Montenegrian army falls back to join the Serbs in the Albanian town of Scutari.

22. Austro-Hungarians capture Scutari. The Montenegrians and Serbs march south to the port of Valona.

Hussein, Sherif of Mecca, will rebel against the Turks if sent weapons by Britain.

4. British forces leave Basra to relieve Kut.

8. Gallipoli. Allied evacuation is completed.

10. Russia invades Turkey at Erzerum.

1. British forces capture Yaunde, capital of the German colony of Cameroons.

GERMANS ATTACK VERDUN

PORTUGAL JOINS THE WAR

WESTERN FRONT

⚜ 1. Seven German Zeppelin airships launch the largest air raid on Britain so far.

♟ 14. British and French commanders agree to begin their major offensive on 1 July.

⚜ 21. Verdun. A German artillery barrage is followed by an attack with 150,000 men.

⚜ 24. Verdun. German troops break the second of three lines of French defences.

⚜ 25. Verdun. French commander General Henri-Philippe Pétain takes command. He states, "They shall not pass."

⚜ 2. Verdun. French forts Vaux and Douaumont are now in German hands.

🤝 9. Germany declares war on Portugal.

▲ *HMS* Dreadnought. *By 1914, the most modern warships were encased in thick armour and carried large guns mounted in armoured turrets that could turn to face different directions.*

EASTERN FRONT

⚜ 18. Battle of Lake Naroch. Russian attack with 350,000 men begins against 75,000 Germans near Vilna.

⚜ 9. The British navy transports the surviving Montenegrian and Serb soldiers to Salonika.

THE MED AND MIDDLE EAST

⚜ 16. Russian troops advance from Erzerum into Turkish Armenia. Armenian rebels tell him that one million Armenians have been massacred by the Turks. The Turks say that only a few thousand rebels were killed in fighting and all civilians were spared.

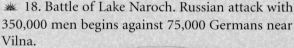

▲ *A motor ambulance with the driver's seat protected by covers. Wounded men evacuated quickly stood a much better chance of survival, so these vehicles were in high demand.*

⚜ 2. Fifth Battle of Isonzo. An Italian offensive fails against the Austro-Hungarians.

⚜ 11. British advance on Kut is halted.

REST OF THE WORLD

🤝 23. Portugal objects to German attacks on neutral shipping and announces that all Portuguese ports, including colonial ports, are closed to German ships.

KEY 🤝 DIPLOMACY ♟ HOME ♠ NAVAL ♟ SECRET WAR ⚜ BATTLE

THE BRITISH AT KUT SURRENDER TO THE TURKS

WESTERN FRONT

☀ 9. Verdun. Renewed German assaults begin on Dead Man Ridge. French losses rise alarmingly under attack from German artillery and poison gas.

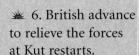 21. The Easter Rising. Irish nationalists start a rebellion in Dublin aimed at achieving Irish independence from Britain.

EASTERN FRONT

☀ 14. Battle of Lake Naroch. Russian attack is called off by Tzar Nicholas II after suffering 122,000 casualties, compared to 20,000 German losses.

▲ Irish rebels defend ruined buildings in Dublin against British troops armed with machine guns.

◄ The British army of 1916 was made up of well-equipped volunteers. The uniform of a soldier consisted of a steel helmet to protect the head from shrapnel, lengths of cloth called puttees worn around the legs to protect from mud, waterproof boots and a tunic. Each soldier also carried a rifle and a bayonet. Bayonets were only used in close combat.

THE MED AND MIDDLE EAST

☀ 6. British advance to relieve the forces at Kut restarts.

☀ 18. Russian troops capture key port of Trebizond in Turkey.

☀ 29. British forces at Kut surrender.

REST OF THE WORLD

ARAB REVOLT BEGINS   BRUSILOV OFFENSIVE BEGINS

WESTERN FRONT

🎩 1. The Easter Rising. The British crush the Irish rebellion in Dublin and execute 14 rebels.

⚜ 1. Verdun. New French commander General Robert Nivelle begins to plan counteroffensive.

⚜ 2. Another major raid by eight German Zeppelin airships hits ports along the East Coast.

⚜ 23. Verdun. Renewed German attack near Fort Vaux moves towards Fort Souville, which dominates the only supply route open to the French in Verdun.

⚜ 24. Battle of the Somme. Around 2000 British artillery guns open fire on German defences around the river Somme, firing an estimated 1.5 million shells each day for the next six days.

EASTERN FRONT

⚜ 4. The Brusilov Offensive begins as Russian troops attack on a 320-km-wide front against Austro-Hungarians south of the Pripet Marshes, led by General Aleksey Brusilov. Brusilov devises new tactics.

⚜ 10. The Brusilov Offensive. Austro-Hungarian armies collapse at Lutsk and Kovel.

⚜ 18. The Brusilov Offensive. German reinforcements slow down the Russian attack, but fail to stop Brusilov's advance.

THE MED AND MIDDLE EAST

⚜ 2. Multinational Allied force marches from Salonika towards the Serb border.

⚜ 5. Hussein of Mecca starts the Arab Revolt.

⚜ 15. A major Austro-Hungarian attack at Trentino smashes the Italian 1st Army.

🤝 3. The Allied force at Salonika arrests Greek officials. Greece mobilizes its army.

⚜ 8. Austro-Hungarian attack is halted due to supply problems in the Alps.

REST OF THE WORLD

🤝 14. China agrees to allow the Allies to recruit labourers to work on construction projects.

⚓ 31. Battle of Jutland. The main British and German warfleets clash in the North Sea.

⚓ 1. Battle of Jutland. German fleet returns to port due to severe damage, despite sinking several British warships. The Germans never again dare face the British fleet.

BATTLE OF THE SOMME BEGINS

☀ 1. Battle of the Somme. The British, supported by the French, advance on a 40-km-wide front around the river Somme. Despite a heavy artillery bombardment, the strong German defences are mostly intact. By nightfall the British have suffered almost 60,000 casualties, 20,000 of them killed. The Germans have lost just 8000 men.

☀ 2. Battle of the Somme. British commander Douglas Haig, misled by early reports, orders massive new attacks to take place, causing more heavy casualties.

☀ 3. Battle of the Somme. British commander Douglas Haig orders new attacks, but heavy rain makes them impossible. Haig later learns of the massive losses and small advances achieved. He orders a halt to the attacks.

☀ 14. Battle of the Somme. Haig orders fresh British attacks on a smaller scale. Local successes encourage him to extend the concept of small, sudden attacks.

☀ 23. Battle of the Somme. The new British tactics lead to the capture of Pozières, but a major breakthrough is not achieved.

☀ 25. Brusilov Offensive. The Russians renew the attack, but are now faced by fresh German forces. The Russians continue to advance, but at a slower rate and for higher casualties.

▲ *French troops race forwards across the smooth, grassy fields of the Somme area. French attacks in the south proved more successful than those of the British.*

BRITISH ATTACKS ON THE SOMME CONTINUE

🎈 2. A major raid by Zeppelin airships on England ends when one is shot down.

🎩 13. Battle of the Somme. British commander Douglas Haig writes to the British government accepting that he will not break through the German defences, but promising to continue the smaller attacks to wear down German defences.

🎩 28. Battle of the Somme. General Haig is ordered to mount a new attack to tie down German reserves on the Somme so that they cannot be moved to attack Romania.

🎈 29. General Erich von Falkenhayn is replaced by Field Marshal Paul von Hindenburg as German Chief of the General Staff in overall command of the war. Hindenburg meets with German industrialists with the aim of tripling the output of weapons and ammunition within six months.

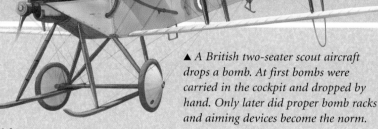

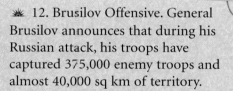

▲ *A British two-seater scout aircraft drops a bomb. At first bombs were carried in the cockpit and dropped by hand. Only later did proper bomb racks and aiming devices become the norm.*

⚔ 12. Brusilov Offensive. General Brusilov announces that during his Russian attack, his troops have captured 375,000 enemy troops and almost 40,000 sq km of territory.

🎩 17. Russian secret agents open talks with King Ferdinand of Romania, using Brusilov's announcement as proof that the Russians would win the war. They hope to persuade King Ferdinand to attack Bulgaria.

⚔ 17. Bulgarian troops invade Greece to attack Allied forces around Salonika.

🤝 27. King Ferdinand of Romania decides to join the Allies. Romania declares war on Austria–Hungary and invades Transylvania, which has a large ethnic Romanian population.

🤝 29. Germany and Bulgaria declare war on Romania.

⚔ 4. Sixth Battle of the Isonzo. Italian troops finally take the ruins of Gorizia, their main target of the previous summer.

⚔ 4. Anzac troops halt a renewed Turkish attack on the Suez Canal.

⚔ 5. In Armenia, the Turks capture Mus.

🤝 28. Italy declares war on Germany.

🎩 17. British codebreakers intercept German radio signals that reveal a force of German warships is to attack the British town of Sunderland. The British fleet is ordered to sea.

⚓ 19. German U-boats sight the British fleet and sink two cruisers. The German fleet turns back to Germany rather than risk a major battle.

TANKS ENTER WARFARE

LAWRENCE OF ARABIA

WESTERN FRONT

3. Battle of the Somme. The fresh British attack takes place at Guillemont and High Wood.

8. Hindenburg visits the Somme and Verdun. He is appalled by the scale of German casualties and issues new orders that positions should be abandoned if they become too costly to defend.

15. Battle of the Somme. The British use tanks for the first time, but most break down.

5. The French government temporarily nationalizes all agricultural land to increase food output.

24. Verdun. A major French offensive begins in dense fog, which masks the attackers from German artillery and machine guns. The attack is aimed at pushing German artillery out of range of Verdun. On the first day, the French capture Fort Douaumont and 6000 prisoners.

◄ *Injured British and German soldiers walk away from the Somme battlefield to British first aid posts behind the front lines.*

EASTERN FRONT

3. A joint German–Bulgarian army invades Romania from the south.

3. Allied forces at Salonika push invading Bulgarian forces out of Greece.

16. The German–Bulgarian invasion of Romania is halted to secure supply lines.

10. Brusilov Offensive. Tzar Nicholas II orders the end to the Russian attacks as tough German resistance makes the assaults too costly.

19. The German–Bulgarian invasion of Romania restarts along the Black Sea coast.

22. German troops capture the key Romanian port of Constanza on the Black Sea coast.

THE MED AND MIDDLE EAST

14. Seventh Battle of the Isonzo. The Italians launch a short, three-day battle that succeeds in capturing limited objectives.

17. Anzac troops drive the Turks back 50 km from the Suez Canal.

9. Eighth Battle of the Isonzo. The Italians launch another short attack with limited objectives, but this time fail to take them.

16. British officer T E Lawrence takes over as British liaison officer with the Arabs.

REST OF THE WORLD

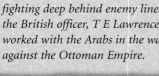

► *Dressed in Arab costume and fighting deep behind enemy lines, the British officer, T E Lawrence, worked with the Arabs in the war against the Ottoman Empire.*

6. Germany announces that it will again sink all merchant ships heading for British ports, including those of neutral countries.

   KEY   🐾 DIPLOMACY   ⚱ HOME   ⚓ NAVAL   ⚒ SECRET WAR   ⚔ BATTLE

VERDUN AND SOMME END

GERMANY'S PEACE NOTE

✼ 2. Verdun. The Germans retreat from several exposed positions, including Fort Vaux.

✼ 12. Battle of the Somme. A fresh British attack, lasting five days, captures Beaumont Hamel, an objective of the attack on 1 July.

🕯 15. The German government announces the early call up of men due to be conscripted in 1918.

✼ 18. Battle of the Somme ends.

✼ 18. Verdun. A final French attack by General Nivelle recaptures most of the land lost.

🕯 5. British Prime Minister Herbert Asquith resigns due to heavy losses and lack of success. The new prime minister is David Lloyd George.

🕯 12. The French government sacks General Joffre as commander in chief and replaces him with General Nivelle, who organized the successful counter attacks at Verdun.

🤝 12. The Peace Note. Germany sends a diplomatic note to all its enemies proposing peace, but on German terms.

🤝 30. The Peace Note is rejected.

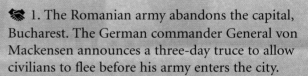

▶ Lloyd George, revolutionized the British armaments industry in 1915, ensuring that the army had enough weapons and ammunition to continue the war.

🤝 5. Germany and Austria–Hungary announce that Polish-speaking areas of Russia are to be an independent country. Thousands of Poles join the German army.

✼ 23. A second German–Bulgarian invasion of Romania begins over the river Danube, while a third crosses the Transylvanian mountains from Austria–Hungary. Both forces make rapid progress as the 500,000-strong Romanian army retreats in confusion.

🤝 1. The Romanian army abandons the capital, Bucharest. The German commander General von Mackensen announces a three-day truce to allow civilians to flee before his army enters the city.

✼ 6. The German army holds a victory parade in Bucharest, then begins to pursue the Romanian army, retreating towards the Russian border.

✼ 1. Ninth Battle of the Isonzo. The Italians begin an attack similar to that in October, with similar disappointing results.

🤝 4. Hussein is crowned King of Mecca.

🤝 23. Greece declares war on Bulgaria.

✼ 13. A fresh British advance in Mesopotamia begins. The advance of 50,000 men is supported by river transports, some converted to be armoured gunboats. Only 20,000 Turks oppose them.

🤝 13. Germany asks Mexico for permission to use Mexican ports to supply U-boats. Mexico refuses.

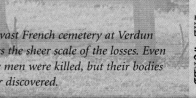

◀ A vast French cemetery at Verdun shows the sheer scale of the losses. Even more men were killed, but their bodies never discovered.

1917

The fighting countries face exhaustion as losses and costs rise.

ZIMMERMANN TELEGRAM

▲ *The Victoria Cross is the highest award for bravery given to British servicemen and women.*

⚔ 9. Battle of Magruntein. British forces drive Turks out of western Sinai.

🤝 19. Zimmermann Telegram. German foreign minister, Zimmermann, sends a telegram suggesting Mexico should attack the USA to recover lands lost in the 19th century.

UNRESTRICTED U-BOAT WARFARE

RUSSIAN REVOLUTION

🌿 23. German forces along the Western Front start withdrawing from the line of trenches. As they fall back, they demolish all buildings and plant mines. The British and French troops advance cautiously over territory that they have fought hard to win. The Germans halt their retreat after 30 km on a line of strong prepared defences known as 'The Hindenburg Line'.

🤝 24. British diplomats hand the US ambassador an intercepted copy of the Zimmermann Telegram.

🕯 German airmen spot signs of massive French preparations for an assault in the Aisne and Champagne region along a 60-km front. A German spy captures the top secret documents, revealing details of the planned French assault. The French attack is later named 'Nivelle's Offensive' after the general who planned it.

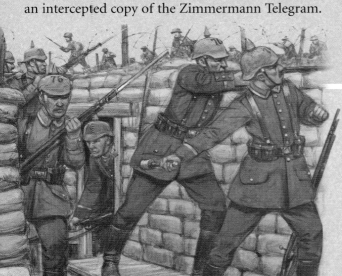

🕯 8. The March Revolution begins in Russia. A wave of strikes and riots break out in major cities, protesting against food shortages and massive war casualties. The army garrison of Petrograd refuses orders to open fire on rioters.

🕯 15. The March Revolution. Chaos spreads rapidly across Russia. After failing to control the situation, Tzar Nicholas II abdicates. The Duma (parliament) establishes a republic with a provisional government led by Alexander Kerensky.

▲ *German infantry occupy a front line trench to repel a British attack. Not all trenches were as well built as this, though the German trenches were generally the best.*

🌿 22. Second Battle of Kut. British forces defeat Turks. Turkish commander Kara Bey orders his forces to withdraw towards Baghdad.

🌿 11. Advancing from Kut-el-Armana, British forces occupy Baghdad.

🌿 26. Advancing from Egypt, British forces attack Gaza in order to invade Palestine, but are driven off and suffer from water shortages.

🤝 3. Germany announces that it will sink all merchant ships without warning. China, USA and others cut diplomatic links to Germany.

🤝 1. The Zimmermann Telegram is published in the USA, stoking anti-German feeling. US President Woodrow Wilson announces that US merchant ships will be armed against U-boats.

USA JOINS THE ALLIES   FRENCH ARMY MUTINIES

WESTERN FRONT

⚔ Bloody April. German pilots in new Albatross DIII fighters destroy almost 30 percent of Allied aircraft on the Western Front.

⚔ 9. Battle of Arras. Canadian troops capture Vimy Ridge, but other British assaults fail to advance very far.

⚔ 16. Nivelle's Offensive. Over 100,000 French soldiers attack prepared German defences. Casualties are high.

⚔ 17. Nivelle's Offensive. The French 108th Regiment refuses to attack. The mutiny spreads rapidly.

🔒 1 Nivelle's Offensive. The French army mutiny that began in April has now spread to 68 of the 112 divisions in the French army. The massive casualties and minor gains of the attack cause widespread alarm. The extent of the rioting and unrest is kept secret.

⚔ 9. Nivelle's Offensive. The offensive is halted – nothing has been achieved and there are 187,000 French casualties. Nivelle is sacked and replaced by General Pétain. Pétain calls off all attacks and concentrates on restoring morale and discipline.

▼ *British soldiers cross a wrecked canal on a narrow wooden bridge.*

EASTERN FRONT

🏠 The March Revolution. The Russian army is paralysed by the upheavals taking place behind its back.

THE MED AND MIDDLE EAST

⚔ 17. A renewed British attack on the Turkish forces at Gaza is again defeated with heavy losses. The British commanders are sacked by the furious Prime Minister Lloyd George.

⚔ 9. Serb and French troops at Salonika attack Macedonia, but make little progress in two weeks of fighting.

⚔ 12. Tenth Battle of the Isonzo. Italian forces once again fail to break through.

REST OF THE WORLD

🤝 6. The USA declares war on Germany following the sinking of several US merchant ships by U-boats.

⚓ 10. The British Royal Navy forces all merchant ships in the North Atlantic to travel in escorted convoys. Losses to German U-boats fall dramatically.

MESSINES RIDGE

⚜ 7. Organized by the innovative General Herbert Plummer, the British 2nd Army captures the strategic Messines Ridge with relatively few losses.

⚜ 14. First German air raid in London by bomber planes.

🔥 24. The first US troops land in France, commanded by General John Pershing. They begin several weeks of training in trench warfare before they enter the front line.

▼ *Aircraft markings. By 1915, the pilots of each nation were painting symbols on their aircraft to help identify friend from foe. The Allies chose round symbols, the Central Powers chose crosses.*

Russia

Belgium

🔥 4. The new Russian Republican government appoints General Alexi Brusilov as the new army commander in chief with orders to stabilize the front and reform the army.

USA

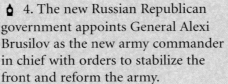

France

Britain

Germany

🔥 13. King Constantine of Greece is forced to abdicate in favour of his son, Alexander, who favours the Allied cause. Eleutherios Venizelos becomes prime minister.

🤝 27. Greece joins the Allies.

Japan

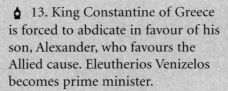

Bulgaria

WESTERN FRONT

EASTERN FRONT

THE MED AND MIDDLE EAST

REST OF THE WORLD

BATTLE OF PASSCHENDAELE BEGINS

WESTERN FRONT

⚜ 13. Battle of Passchendaele. The British offensive begins with massed air attacks to drive the Germans from the skies, followed by a massive two-week artillery barrage.

🎩 24. Dutch-born dancer Mata Hari is put on trial by the French as a German spy. The glamorous international star of the stage is found guilty and executed.

⚜ 31. Battle of Passchendaele. The British offensive begins to the north of Ypres, near Passchendaele, with the aim of breaking through to the coast.

▼ *A British pilot in his Sopwith fighter watches a burning German Albatros pass by. Most pilots did not have parachutes, so combats were often fatal.*

EASTERN FRONT

⚜ 1. Kerensky Offensive. Ordered by Russian Defence Minister Alexander Kerensky, the new Russian defence minister, a fresh offensive takes the Germans and Austro-Hungarians by surprise. The Russians begin well, but the attack falters as resistance stiffens.

⚜ 19. Kerensky Offensive. A German counter attack drives back the Russian army, which begins to disintegrate. Fresh Romanian troops are rushed up to halt the German attack.

THE MED AND MIDDLE EAST

REST OF THE WORLD

ITALIAN VICTORY

RAIN AT PASSCHENDAELE

⚜ 2. Battle of Passchendaele. Sudden and unexpected heavy storms and torrential rain halt the British attack as the low-lying ground around Passchendaele turns to mud.

⚜ 16. Battle of Passchendaele. With dry ground, the British attack begins again, but the element of surprise has been lost and the Germans are ready. Progress is slow and casualties are high. Once again, Haig reverts to his tactic of limited objectives and small-scale attacks.

⚜ 18. Battle of Passchendaele. British commander Haig orders a new attack by Plummer's 2nd Army on the higher, drier ground south of Ypres. Plummer uses new tactics and gains key hills before more heavy rain again turns the area into thick mud. Haig orders the attacks to continue, but the mud makes supply and movement difficult.

⚱ 4. The Russian Republican government, now with Kerensky as prime minister, sacks General Brusilov as the commander in chief and replaces him with General Lavr Kornilov. Kornilov has orders to stop the mutinies, desertions and rebellions that are afflicting the Russian army.

⚜ 1. Using new 'stormtrooper' tactics, the Germans attack towards Riga. The Russian 12th Army collapses, allowing the Germans to sweep forwards with few casualties.

⚱ 9. Russian commander Lavr Kornilov uses the army to mount a coup against the republican government. The coup fails when armed workers attack the few soldiers who support Kornilov. The victory by the workers militia gives added power and prestige to the Bolshevik Communists.

⚜ 12. Eleventh Battle of the Isonzo. A new attack sees Italian forces finally break through towards Trieste. The Austro-Hungarians manage to halt the drive, but realize their armies are exhausted and appeal to Germany for help in any future battle.

⚜ 27. Battle of Ramadi. British forces advancing northwest from Baghdad defeat the local Turkish forces, then continue along the river Tigris.

BRAZIL JOINS THE ALLIES

RUSSIAN REVOLUTION

WESTERN FRONT

🌾 9. Battle of Passchendaele. British commander Haig decides to limit his offensive to the capture of Passchendaele Ridge. A three-day attack by Australian troops begins, but ends in failure.

🌾 28. Battle of Passchendaele. The British make a renewed assault on Passchendaele Ridge, spearheaded by Canadian troops. Progress is slow and casualties are high, but Haig insists the attacks must continue.

🌾 6. Battle of Passchendaele. British and Canadian troops finally capture and fortify the Passchendaele Ridge. Haig calls off the battle – it has cost him 310,000 casualties, and the Germans 260,000. Haig is criticized for not calling off the attack earlier.

🌾 20. Battle of Cambrai. A small British attack is led by 476 tanks that break through the German lines with ease. However, the tanks run out of fuel and reinforcements are slow in arriving. Within ten days, elite formations of German troops have halted the attack.

▼ Russian soldiers carry red cloths on their bayonets as they drive through the streets to show that they have joined the Communist forces.

EASTERN FRONT

🕯 6. The Russian Revolution. Led by Leon Trotsky and Vladimir Lenin, the Bolshevik Communists launch a successful coup that overthrows the Russian Republican government. Disorder and rioting break out in several cities. Desertion from the army reaches massive proportions. Lenin announces an immediate armistice with the Germans and Austro-Hungarians.

THE MED AND MIDDLE EAST

🌾 24. Battle of Caporetto. A joint German and Austro-Hungarian attack in foggy conditions breaks through the Italian front on the river Isonzo. The Italian commander General Cadorna, orders his men to retreat to the river Tagliamento.

🌾 1. Battle of Beersheba. Australian cavalry capture Beersheba. The British invasion of Palestine begins.

🌾 2. Battle of Caporetto. Germans cross the Tagliamento, causing the Italians to flee so fast, the Germans are unable to keep up.

REST OF THE WORLD

♟ 17. Two German light cruisers attack and destroy a British convoy off Scotland.

🤝 26. Brazil declares war on Germany after Brazilian ships are sunk by U-boats.

🌾 27. Battle of Mahiwa. Colonial British forces defeat the German colonial forces of General von Lettow-Vorbeck in German East Africa. The Germans begin a guerrilla campaign.

JAPAN INVADES RUSSIA

🌾 4. Battle of Cambrai. British commander Haig orders his forces to retreat to prepared defences, abandoning all gains made in the battle. He calls off all major attacks to study the results of this, the first major use of tanks in warfare.

🤝 3. German and Russian diplomats discuss a peace treaty.

🤝 9. Abandoned by the Russians, the Romanians agree a ceasefire with Germany.

🔥 9. The new Communist government nationalizes land in Russia, sparking a revolt by Don Cossack peasants. It is the start of a civil war that will spread to engulf most of Russia.

🌾 1. Battle of Caporetto. New Italian troops dig in along the river Piave, halting the German and Austro-Hungarian advance just outside Venice. Short of supplies, the invaders stop to reorganize.

▲ Tanks were first used in 1916 during the Battle of the Somme, but they were unsuccessful. The technology was developed over the following years, and they became essential in battle.

🌾 27. Battle of Vladivostok. Japan invades eastern Russia to seize the strategic port of Vladivostok.

1918

With Russia out of the war and the USA, many recognize that 1918 will be the decisive year.

RUSSIAN CIVIL WAR SPREADS

⚑ 1. Finland becomes independent of Russia, but soon collapses into civil war between Bolshevik Communists and traditionalist factions.

⚑ 28. Estonia, which has also declared itself to be independent of Russia, is invaded by Bolshevik Russian troops. The Estoninans appeal to the Germans for help. A German army is sent to help, marking an end to the Russian–German ceasefire agreed the previous November.

⚓ 20. Two Turkish warships steam into the Aegean Sea, but are driven back by minefields and air attacks.

🤝 27. A British army is sent from Baghdad to Baku to take control of Russian oilfields.

🤝 8. US President Woodrow Wilson announces his '14 Points for Peace', including self-government for nations and the setting up of an international body to prevent wars.

UKRAINE CONQUERED　RUSSIA SURRENDERS

⚓ German commanders Hindenburg and Ludendorff fear that with the vast industrial might and manpower of the USA, the Allies will have an overwhelming advantage. They plan to defeat France and Britain before the Americans arrive in force, expected to be in autumn 1918. They lay detailed plans for a series of massive offensives in France, but first they need the troops tied down in Russia.

⚔ 21. Operation Michael. After a short, intense artillery bombardment, 63 German divisions attack 26 British divisions south of Arras. The German units are led by elite stormtroopers who infiltrate British defences. The British line collapses on a front 48 km wide.

⚔ 25. Operation Michael. The Germans are 40 km from their start lines.

⚱ 26. French General Ferdinand Foch is appointed supreme commander of all British and French armies on the Western Front.

🤝 18. German diplomats in Brest-Litovsk call off talks with the Russians in protest at the Russian refusal to agree a peace deal.

⚔ 19. The Germans launch a major offensive into the Ukraine to seize the vast and prosperous agricultural area. They hope to commandeer enough food to feed the German civilians, and put pressure on the Russian government to agree a quick peace agreement.

🤝 3. Treaty of Brest-Litovsk. Under pressure of German military advances, the new Bolshevik Communist government of Russia agrees to independence for Poland, Finland, Latvia, Lithuania and Estonia. Germany is to occupy the Ukraine. Germany at once starts moving large numbers of troops to the Western Front.

⚔ 24. The Turks launch a major offensive in Armenia to drive the Russians out of Turkey. The longer term aim is to cross the Caucasus Mountains to seize the oilfields around Baku.

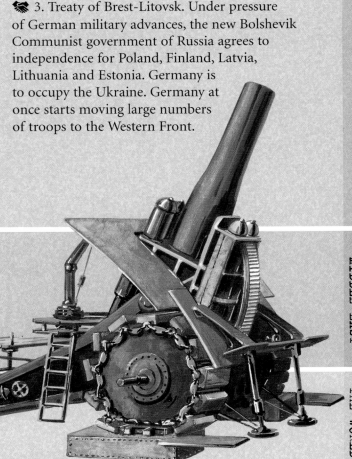

▶ *Shells fired from howitzers fell steeply onto enemy defences, penetrating deep into the soil before exploding.*

GERMAN ATTACK IN WEST   ROMANIA SURRENDERS

WESTERN FRONT

⚜ 5. Operation Michael. The Germans halt their attack as Allied defences strengthen.

⚜ 9. Operation Georgette. The Germans unleash a second massive assault along the river Lys. Portuguese and British defenders fall back in disorder.

⚜ 12. Operation Georgette. British commander Haig orders his men to fight, "with our backs to the wall." By 17 April, the German attacks have been halted.

⚜ 23. Zeebrugge Raid. British amphibious assault destroys a U-boat base at Zeebrugge.

⚜ 27. Operation Blücher. A third German offensive opens as a limited attack on the strategic ridge of Chemin des Dames. French defenders flee in disorder.

⚜ 28. Operation Blücher. US troops in action for the first time hold the key high ground around Cantigny.

⚜ 29. Operation Blücher. German forces capture Soissons, following the fleeing French. The next day the Germans are only 60 km from Paris. German commander Ludendorff decides to pour in extra men.

EASTERN FRONT

🤝 7. Treaty of Bucharest. Romania surrenders to Germany, Austria–Hungary and Bulgaria, which between them occupy 85 percent of Romania. However, King Ferdinand of Romania lives up to his reputation for cunning by finding excuses never to sign the treaty, allowing him to claim that Romania is still a combatant nation when the final peace treaties are being negotiated in 1919.

THE MED AND MIDDLE EAST

▶ Gas balloons carried men equipped with maps and radio sets. The men identified enemy targets for the artillery.

REST OF THE WORLD

KEY 🤝 DIPLOMACY ⌂ HOME ⚓ NAVAL 🗡 SECRET WAR ⚜ BATTLE

GERMAN ATTACKS HALTED   # TSAR OF RUSSIA SHOT

☀ 4. Operation Blücher. German forces are blocked at Chateau Thierry by reorganized French and US defences. Ludendorff halts the offensive.

☀ 9. Operation Gneisenau. German armies attack near Amiens, damaging the French defences.

☀ 13. Operation Gneisenau. The German attack is called off after a successful French counter attack.

☀ 15. German commander Ludendorff begins an attack on the Marne to draw Allied forces away from the north, where he intends to capture the Channel ports. The attack lasts two days, but fails to reach its objectives.

☀ 18. Second Battle of the Marne. A joint French, British and US counter attack takes the Germans by surprise. Ludendorff moves his reserves from the north to halt the new threat.

◄ *The former Tsar Nicholas II with his family while they were prisoners of the Communists.*

🤝 23. Allied troops land at Archangel to supply anti-Communist Russian forces.

🤝 11. Newly independent Lithuania chooses Prince Wilhelm of Urach to be their King under the name of Mindove.

⚱ 16. The former Tzar Nicholas II of Russia and his family are shot dead by Bolshevik Communists who have been holding them prisoner for some months.

⚱ 26. Breaking out of their prison camps in the Urals, a force of Austro-Hungarian soldiers find themselves amid the chaos of the Russian civil war. They begin the journey home.

⚓ 9. Austro-Hungarian battleship Szent Istvan is sunk in battle against the Italians.

☀ 13. Battle of the Piave. A massive Austro-Hungarian attack pushes the Italians back over the Piave, but fails to break through.

🤝 23. Allied troops land at Vladivostok to prevent a Japanese occupation. A force of Austro-Hungarian prisoners break out of the Russian prison camp to help.

THE BLACK DAY

FOURTH BATTLE OF YPRES

WESTERN FRONT

⚝ 2. Second Battle of the Marne. French soldiers recapture Soissons as the Germans fall back towards defences along the river Vesle.

⚝ 8. British forces attack east of Amiens, spearheaded by a large force of tanks. The Germans surrender or retreat without offering any resistance. Ludendorff calls this 'The Black Day of the German army'. The British advance continues for two weeks, when it is halted as supplies can no longer keep up with the advancing troops.

⚝ 3. Expecting further Allied attacks, German General Ludendorff orders a retreat to the Hindenburg Line. The move takes two weeks to complete.

⚝ 26. The Argonne Offensive. A joint French–US attack begins north of Verdun towards Sedan. The Germans are fighting on territory that they have occupied for over three years with strongly defended fortifications. Allied progress is slow.

⚝ 27. Fourth Battle of Ypres. A British advance pushes the Germans back more than 15 km.

EASTERN FRONT

THE MED AND MIDDLE EAST

REST OF THE WORLD

▼ *The main talks at Versailles took place between politicians and soldiers of the victorious states. Each country wanted something different and the talks dragged on for months.*

🤝 14. A large Turkish army arrives at the key Russian oilfields around Baku. The British force that has been occupying the area is driven out.

TURKEY SURRENDERS   THE WAR ENDS

🤝 6. German Prince Max contacts US President Wilson to ask for terms of an armistice.

🎖 14. The Argonne Offensive. The French–US attack captures the final German defences, but halts for reinforcements to arrive.

🎖 22. Fourth Battle of Ypres. The British drive the Germans across the river Selle and continue to advance steadily.

🤝 7. Led by Matthias Erzberger, German diplomats meet French Marshal Foch to discuss an armistice. Foch's demands are so severe that Erzberger contacts Berlin for advice.

🎖 8. The British forces advancing from Ypres cross the river Scheldt, meeting little resistance as German forces surrender or break up.

🏛 9. German Kaiser Wilhelm II abdicates. Germany becomes a republic.

🤝 11. Germany agrees to an armistice. It comes into force at 11 a.m.

🏛 17. German forces march home and disband.

🤝 2. Lithuania ousts its new German king and proclaims itself to be a republic.

🤝 4. Under the terms of the Turkish armistice, the Turkish army occupying the Russian oilfields around Baku surrenders to the British.

🏛 11. Austro-Hungarian Emperor Karl abdicates.

🏛 11. General Jozef Pilsudski becomes the first president of an independent Poland.

🏛 15. Ukraine collapses into civil war as Bolsheviks invade. Civil war spreads across Russia.

🎖 15. British and Arab forces enter Damascus as Turkish forces flee north.

🎖 23. Battle of Vittorio Veneto. Italian armies drive across the river Piave.

🤝 30. Turkey agrees to an armistice one month after Bulgaria.

🤝 4. The Austro-Hungarian government agrees to an armistice with Italy pending the negotiation of a final peace treaty with the other Allies. No peace treaty is ever signed as the Austro-Hungarian Empire ceases to exist.

🏛 29. The Kiel Mutiny. German sailors of the High Seas Fleet at Kiel refuse to obey orders to go to sea.

🏛 25. The final German surrender takes place at Abercorn in Northern Rhodesia when the guerrillas receive news of the armistice and surrender to British colonial troops.

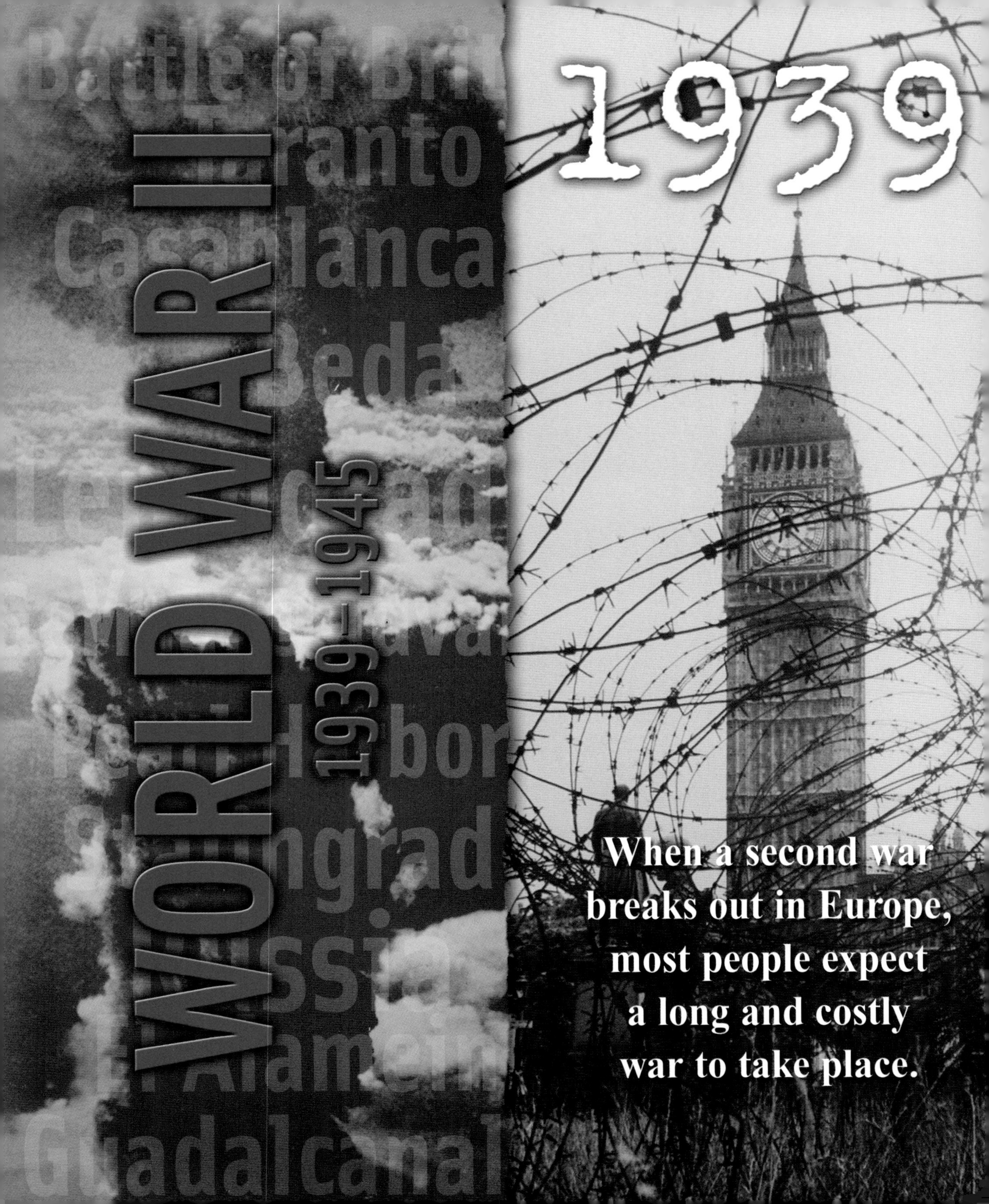

Battle of Bri...

...ranto

Casablanca

...eda...

WORLD WAR II

1939–1945

...avai...

...bor

...ngrad

...ssi...

...lamein

Guadalcanal

1939

When a second war
breaks out in Europe,
most people expect
a long and costly
war to take place.

WAR BREAKS OUT AS GERMANY INVADES POLAND

🤝 1. Denmark, Norway, Finland and Sweden declare themselves neutral.

🤝 3. Britain, France, Australia, New Zealand and India declare war on Germany.

🤝 3. Belgium announces it will remain neutral in any European war.

⚓ 3. First U-boat victim of the war, the British liner *Athenia*. A total of 112 civilians are killed, 28 of them Americans.

🤝 6. South Africa declares war on Germany.

⚔ 7. Battle of the Saar. French forces invade Germany in Saar valley.

🤝 10. Canada declares war on Germany.

⚓ 15. First convoy of merchant ships protected by naval warships sets out from Jamaica for Britain.

⚔ 30. Battle of the Saar. French forces retreat from occupied areas of Germany.

⚓ 30. German battleship *Graf Spee* begins sinking merchant ships in the South Atlantic.

🤝 4. Japan announces it will remain neutral in any European war. Japan is already fighting a war against China.

▶ *In 1938, Germany took over the Sudetenland, signalling the end for the Czechs. Hitler surveys his new territory with high-ranking military escort.*

⚔ 1. Germany invades Poland.

🤝 1. Poland declares war on Germany and appeals to Britain and France for help.

⚔ 9. Battle of the Bzura. Polish counter attack lasting six days fails to halt advance of German panzers on Warsaw.

⚔ 17. Russian invasion of Poland. Soviets seize eastern parts of Poland.

🤝 30. Polish government flees to France.

🤝 1. Italy declares itself neutral in the war between its ally Germany, and Poland.

KEY 🤝 DIPLOMACY 🏠 HOME ⚓ NAVAL 🔦 SECRET WAR ⚔ BATTLE

POLAND SURRENDERS

WESTERN FRONT

🤝 2. All American countries (except Canada) declare themselves neutral and ban fighting warships from entering to within 1000 km of their coasts.

⚓ 5. Britain and France send out naval flotillas to hunt the German battleship *Graf Spee*.

🤝 6. Adolf Hitler offers to convene a 'Peace Conference' with Britain and France. The offer is rejected unless German troops evacuate Poland.

🕵 7. British Expeditionary Force of 161,000 men completes arrival in France.

⚓ 14. German submarine U-47 sinks British battleship HMS *Royal Oak* inside naval base of Scapa Flow.

⚓ 20. Germany announces that merchant ships of any nationality in Allied convoys will be sunk without warning.

EASTERN FRONT

◀ *Hitler emerged from World War I with a vision of Germany reborn and a new German Empire.*

THE MED AND MIDDLE EAST

⚔ 6. Final Polish army surrenders to Germans at Kock, near Warsaw.

🕵 14. Polish agents escape to France with a German Enigma code machine. Work begins on cracking German coded radio signals.

⚔ 16. Germans end Polish campaign.

🕵 24. Polish gold reserves arrive in France.

🤝 28. Soviet leader Josef Stalin demands that Finland hand over border territories.

REST OF THE WORLD

🤝 19. Britain and France sign a treaty of friendship with Turkey.

⚓ 25. Three German U-boats are sent to the Mediterranean to attack Allied shipping.

RUSSIA INVADES FINLAND

RIVER PLATE

🤝 1. The Netherlands declares itself neutral, but mobilizes army and navy.

🤝 7. Belgium and Netherlands issue joint offer of mediation to find a path to peace.

🔥 8. Assassination attempt on Hitler by left-wing activist fails.

⚔ 12. First German air raid on Britain.

🤝 15. Germany rejects Belgian–Dutch offer.

⚔ 9. First British soldier killed in action – Corporal Thomas Priday on patrol in France.

⚔ 13. Battle of the river Plate. Three British cruisers clash with the German battleship *Graf Spee* off South America. *Graf Spee* is damaged and is scuttled four days later.

▶ *Around 2.5 million steel Anderson shelters were issued before September 1939. The roof was covered with soil and grass as camouflage.*

⚔ 27. Japanese capture key transport centre of Nanning in China.

⚔ 28. Japan launches heavy bombing raids on Chinese city of Lanchow in attempt to halt production of ammunition in the city's factories.

🔥 1. Poland is officially partitioned between Germany and Russia.

⚔ 30. Russia invades Finland. Russian armies advance on four fronts and bomb Finnish capital of Helsinki.

⚔ 2. Finnish forces fall back to prepared defences on the Mannerheim Line.

🤝 3. International Olympic Committee cancel 1940 Olympics, due to be held in Finland.

⚔ 16. Finns repel Russian attacks at Summa.

WESTERN FRONT

EASTERN FRONT

THE MED AND MIDDLE EAST

REST OF THE WORLD

1940

Hitler plans to end the war with a Blitzkrieg on France.

RUSSIAN ATTACK HALTED

3. British government takes over all merchant shipping for the duration of the war.

10. German aircraft carrying complete set of plans for German invasion of France lands by mistake in Belgium during a snowstorm. Belgian authorities pass the plans to France. Hitler orders that new plans be drawn up.

29. German air force (*Luftwaffe*) begins campaign against British merchant ships in the North Sea.

31. French government announces second month without major land fighting.

21. *Asama Maru* incident. British warship stops and searches the Japanese merchant ship *Asama Maru*. They find and arrest 21 German weapons technicians. The incident leads to long-running diplomatic dispute between Britain and Japan.

5. Finns surround and destroy Russian 18th Division near Lake Ladoga.

11. Finns crush Russian attack near Salla.

25. Finns repel renewed Russian attacks in the Lake Ladoga area.

21. *Orazio* incident. French warships race to rescue survivors when Italian liner *Orazio* catches fire off Spain.

PHONEY WAR CONTINUES ON LAND, BUT NOT AT SEA

⚜ 8. French patrol captures a German patrol in the Forbach Forest. No other land fighting reported in February.

♟ 9. German destroyers make first of several night voyages to lay mines off the east coast of England.

♟ 12. British navy capture German U-33, complete with code books.

♟ 16. *Altmark* Incident. British warships pursue German merchant ship *Altmark* into Norwegian waters to rescue British prisoners. Norway objects.

◀ *Scanning the skies, a 'spotter' uses binoculars to look for enemy planes approaching London.*

⚜ 1. Battle of Sama. Major Russian assault begins on the Mannerheim Line at Sama.

⚜ 16. Battle of Sama. Finns withdraw to new defensive positions having inflicted huge losses on the Russians.

KEY 🤝 DIPLOMACY 🏠 HOME ♟ NAVAL 🕵 SECRET WAR ⚜ BATTLE

FINLAND SURRENDERS TO RUSSIA

WESTERN FRONT

⚔ 2. Germans capture British patrol on the Franco-German border.

⬥ 11. Britain introduces rationing of meat.

⚔ 16. Germans launch major air raid on British naval base at Scapa Flow. One cruiser is badly damaged.

⚔ 17. British launch reprisal air raid on German naval base at Sylt. No serious damage is caused.

⬥ 20. French government falls over criticism of policy towards Finland. New Prime Minister is Paul Reynaud.

⚔ 24. German patrols active along entire Western Front. French respond with artillery fire on German positions.

🕳 28. British government agrees to suggestion by First Lord of the Admiralty, Winston Churchill, that neutral Norwegian waters should be mined to stop merchant ships carrying iron ore to Germany. France objects, then agrees only if the move is delayed by one week.

▶ *In Britain, ration books became part of everyone's daily life, along with an identity card.*

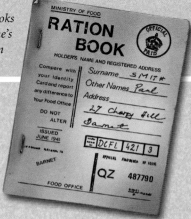

EASTERN FRONT

◀ *Mussolini, Italy's Fascist leader, dreamt of a new Roman Empire. The name 'Fascism' comes from the Latin word 'fasces', which were bundles of rods carried before magistrates in ancient Rome.*

THE MED AND MIDDLE EAST

⚔ 1. Battle of Viipuri. Largest Russian attack of the Finnish War opens with determined assaults on the city of Viipuri.

⚔ 10. Battle of Viipuri. Final Finnish reserves committed. Marshal Mannerheim advises Finnish government to make peace.

🤝 12. Treaty of Moscow. Finland retains independence, but hands over extensive border territory to Russia.

REST OF THE WORLD

⚓ 7. British Mediterranean Fleet seizes Italian coal ships. Diplomatic row ends with ships being returned to Italy, but Britain retains right to search Italian ships.

🤝 18. Hitler and Mussolini meet at Brenner. Mussolini is vague about joining the war.

GERMANY INVADES DENMARK AND NORWAY

⚔ 2. German air raid on British naval bases.

♠ 7. British ships leave to begin mining Norwegian waters.

♠ 8. British destroyer *Glowworm* meets major German naval fleet off Norway and is sunk.

⚔ 9. Germany invades Denmark.

⚔ 9. Germany invades Norway. Norwegian artillery sinks German battle-cruiser *Blücher* off Oslo. British and German warships exchange fire off Narvik and Kristiansand.

🤝 10. Denmark surrenders to Germany. Iceland declares itself independent of Denmark.

⚔ 13. Battle of Narvik. British battleship *Warspite* sinks eight German destroyers.

⚔ 14. British troops land near Narvik.

🤝 15. King Haakon of Norway says he will, "save the freedom of our beloved country."

⚔ 17. British warships begin to bombard German coastal positions in Norway.

⚔ 26. Norwegians halt German advance along Gudbrandsbal Valley.

♠ 3. Two Russian merchant ships arrive in Hong Kong under escort by British warships. The ships are carrying cargoes that the British believe is to be transported along the Trans-Siberian Railway to Germany. Russia objects. The British release the ships, but retain the cargoes.

🔥 1. More than 450,000 Finns are expelled from occupied areas by Russians. They are marched to Helsinki and all their possessions confiscated by the Russian government.

▶ *Churchill, in RAF uniform, displaying his infamous 'V' for Victory sign. His hope in 1940 was that the USA would soon join the war to tilt the balance.*

GERMANY INVADES BELGIUM, NETHERLANDS AND FRANCE

WESTERN FRONT

6. Norway's gold reserves arrive in Britain.

7. British Parliament debates the conduct of the war. Prime Minister Neville Chamberlain is severely criticized and three days later resigns to be replaced by Winston Churchill.

10. Germany invades Belgium, Netherlands and Luxembourg. British and French armies march into Belgium.

12. Fresh French troops land at Narvik.

13. German panzers cross the river Meuse at Sedan and Dinant opening a gap 80 km wide in the French defences.

14. Central Rotterdam is destroyed by German bombing.

14. The Netherlands surrender to Germany.

20. German panzers reach the Channel coast at Abbéville. British retreat begins.

26. Operation Dynamo. Evacuation of British and French troops from Dunkirk begins under heavy attack by *Luftwaffe*.

28. Belgium surrenders to Germany.

EASTERN FRONT

11. Japan warns that it will not tolerate occupation of the Dutch East Indies (Indonesia) by the armed forces of any nation other than the Netherlands.

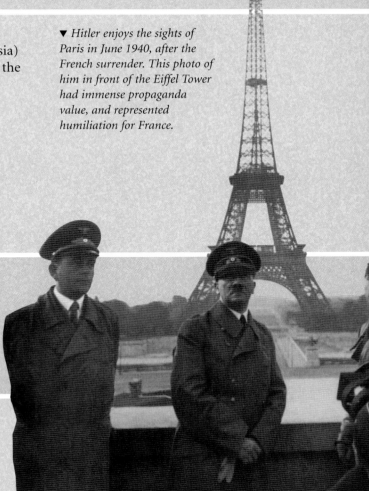

▼ *Hitler enjoys the sights of Paris in June 1940, after the French surrender. This photo of him in front of the Eiffel Tower had immense propaganda value, and represented humiliation for France.*

THE MED AND MIDDLE EAST

REST OF THE WORLD

26. Benito Mussolini believes Germany will win the war. He decides to join Germany, hoping to gain glory and diplomatic advantage.

NORWAY AND FRANCE SURRENDER TO GERMANY

⚜ 3. Operation Dynamo ends. In all, 210,000 British and 120,000 French troops are successfully evacuated from Dunkirk.

⚜ 5. Battle of France. Reorganized German forces strike in the south over the Somme. French front collapses after 24 hours.

⚜ 8. Battle of France. German panzer spearheads reach the river Seine.

⚑ 8. King Haakon leaves Norway for Britain.

🤝 9. Norwegian army surrenders. Norwegian navy to continue the war from Britain.

⚜ 14. Battle of France. Germans march into Paris, which is undefended by the French.

⚜ 14. Battle of France. French resistance collapses. German panzers advance 250 km in one day.

🕯 16. New French government formed under Marshal Pétain, hero of World War I.

🕯 18. French warships leave France for ports in French colonies.

🤝 22. France surrenders.

⚜ 14. Japanese air force begins series of fire bomb raids on Chinese city of Chungking.

⚜ 15. Russia invades Lithuania without declaring war.

⚜ 17. Russia invades Latvia and Estonia without declaring war.

⚜ 28. Russia invades Romania without declaring war.

🤝 Romania surrenders after three days. Border provinces of Bessarabia and Bukovina are annexed to Russia.

🤝 30. Communist governments are imposed on Lithuania, Estonia and Latvia by Russia.

🤝 10. Italy declares war on France and Britain. Italians invade southern France.

⚜ 14. Italian warships shell British coastal positions in Egypt.

⚜ 23. Italians capture French city of Menton.

⚜ 28. Air fights take place between Italian and British forces over Libyan–Egyptian border.

HITLER OFFERS PEACE

BATTLE OF BRITAIN BEGINS

WESTERN FRONT

🍾 1. French government sets up office in Vichy. Most of northern and western France is occupied by the Germans.

⚓ 3. Britain seizes all French ships in British and colonial ports, including 59 warships.

💥 10. Battle of Britain. Massed German air attacks on British ports and shipping begin.

🤝 19. Hitler offers peace to Britain. The offer is rejected.

🍾 21. Britain forms the Home Guard, a voluntary local defence militia.

🔨 1. Hitler sets 15 September as date for invasion of Britain.

💥 10. Battle of Britain. Massed German air attacks on British ports and shipping reach a peak, then strikes begin on RAF bases.

💥 15. Battle of Britain. Heaviest German air attacks yet pound RAF bases across Britain.

💥 16. Battle of Britain. RAF base at Tangmere is put out of action by German attacks.

💥 24. Battle of Britain. RAF base at Manton is put out of action by German attacks.

EASTERN FRONT

🤝 19. Under pressure from Japan, British authorities in Burma, a British colony, agree to stop military supplies passing through Burma to China.

🤝 25. Britain withdraws its small garrisons from various Chinese towns, such as Shanghai and Tientsin. The garrisons had been introduced to ensure the safety of British merchants and goods. However, trade has collapsed since the China–Japan war began and the men are needed elsewhere.

THE MED AND MIDDLE EAST

🍾 4. Under pressure from Germany, Romania expels the British from the oil fields.

🤝 21. Communist parliaments in Estonia, Latvia and Lithuania vote to join USSR.

🤝 21. Bulgaria takes Dobrudja from Romania.

REST OF THE WORLD

⚓ 3. British warships sink French warships at Mers-el-Kebir to prevent their capture.

⚓ 19. Battle of Cape Spada. The British sink one Italian cruiser, but sustain heavy damage.

💥 3. Italians invade British colonies of Sudan and Somaliland from Ethiopia.

💥 20. Italians begin blockade of Malta.

KEY 🤝 DIPLOMACY 🍾 HOME ⚓ NAVAL 🔨 SECRET WAR 💥 BATTLE

▶ An aerial 'dogfight'. RAF Spitfires attack German Heinkel bombers, with Messerschmitt Bf 109 fighter escorts. For a few minutes the air is crowded with twisting, diving planes, machine guns chattering.

WESTERN FRONT

EASTERN FRONT

THE MED AND MIDDLE EAST

REST OF THE WORLD

ITALY INVADES EGYPT   BATTLE OF BRITAIN ENDS

WESTERN FRONT

⚜ 1. Battle of Britain. Major German attacks on RAF bases continue. British losses are heavy.

⚜ 7. The Blitz. First major air raid on London.

⚜ 14. Battle of Britain. British bombers attack German invasion fleet in Belgian ports.

⚜ 15. Battle of Britain. Largest German attacks of the battle take place day and night.

⚜ 17. Hitler abandons invasion of Britain.

⚓ 20. 'Wolf Pack' tactics by German U-boats gain first success with sinking of 12 ships from British convoy HX72 in a single night.

⚜ 4. The Blitz. Night raid on London by 130 German bombers. Raids continue on London and other cities almost every night throughout the autumn and winter.

⚜ 14. The Blitz. RAF bombs Berlin. *Luftwaffe* bombs London.

⚓ 17. British and German destroyers clash off the Cornish coast.

🤝 23. Hitler meets with Spanish dictator General Franco in the Pyrenees. Franco expresses support, but refuses to join the war.

EASTERN FRONT

⚜ 13. Japanese bomb Chungking, using the Zero fighter for the first time.

🤝 22. Vichy French government agrees to Japanese demand to use air and naval bases in French colonies of Indo-China (now Vietnam, Laos and Cambodia). French garrison at Da Nang refuse to comply and fighting breaks out.

🤝 27. Japan signs the political and economic Tripartite Pact with Germany and Italy.

▼ *The Germans sent waves of bombers and fighters from bases in occupied Europe to attack London and other cities. Here London's docks burn with Tower Bridge unscathed.*

THE MED AND MIDDLE EAST

REST OF THE WORLD

⚜ 13. Italians invade Egypt from Libya. The British fall back to prepared defences.

⚜ 17. Italian advance into Egypt halts at Sidi Barrani.

⚓ 1. British cruisers break Italian blockade to land troops and supplies on Malta.

⚜ 28. Italy invades Greece at three points from Italian-occupied Albania.

BATTLE OF TARANTO

ITALY DEFEATED IN GREECE

⚓ 5. German battleship *Admiral Scheer* attacks British Atlantic convoy, sinking six ships. All convoys cancelled for two weeks.

☀ 14. Massed attack by 440 German aircraft on Coventry guided by new navigational equipment destroys the city centre, burns the medieval cathedral and kills 600 people.

☀ 19. Heavy raid by German aircraft on Birmingham leaves 3000 dead or injured.

☀ 28. Heavy raid by German aircraft on Liverpool is thwarted by navigational problems.

☀ 12. Heavy raid by German aircraft on Sheffield badly hits iron foundries.

☀ 16. RAF launch 'area' raid on Mannheim. One aircraft bombs Basle in Switzerland.

⚓ 25. German cruiser *Admiral Hipper* attacks British Atlantic convoy off Spain, but is driven off by British cruiser *Berwick*.

☀ 29. *Luftwaffe* drop 30,000 incendiary bombs on central London. Large areas of the historic city go up in flames.

⚓ Allies lost 1059 merchant ships in 1940.

▶ *Franco, a national hero after army service in Spain's North African colonies, led the Nationalists to victory, and ruled as dictator of Spain until his death in 1975.*

⚓ 9. German raider *Passat* lays mines off Australian coast, sinking two merchant ships. Port of Melbourne is closed until minesweepers can be brought into action.

⚓ 21. German raider *Komet* lands prisoners taken from sunk merchant ships on the remote island of Emirau, then radios the location to the Australian navy to arrange rescue.

🤝 20. Hungary signs military alliance with Germany and Italy.

🤝 22. Romania signs military alliance with Germany, Italy and Hungary. Romania wants to regain lands annexed by Russia.

🤝 12. Hungary signs friendship treaty with Yugoslavia.

✒ 18. Hitler orders his military staff to draw up plans for a German invasion of Russia to start in June.

☀ 3. Greeks halt Italian attacks in the Pindus Mountains, but fall back on the coast.

⚓ 11. British naval aircraft attack Taranto, crippling three Italian battleships.

🫙 1. Italy begins rationing of pasta.

☀ 3. Greeks drive Italians into Albania.

☀ 9. British launch surprise attack at Sidi Barrani. Italians retreat back to Libya.

1941

The war spreads to engulf Russia, Japan and the USA.

CONVOYS THREATENED

⚜ 3. Night raid by *Luftwaffe* on Bristol destroys huge stocks of grain and flour.

🤝 9. Senior US diplomat, Harry Hopkins, arrives in Britain on a mission from US President Roosevelt to discuss how the USA can help Britain.

⚜ 10. *Luftwaffe* drop incendiary bombs on Portsmouth, destroying large area of town.

♟ 22. Powerful German warships *Gneisenau* and *Scharnhorst* leave Kiel. They evade British patrols in the North Sea and enter the Atlantic to attack British shipping.

♟ 17. Battle of Koh Chang. Attempted Thai invasion of French Indo-China halted when Vichy French fleet crushes Thai fleet, sinking three ships.

▶ *Barrage balloons rose on their cables in their hundreds above key targets, such as airfields and armament factories.*

♟ 21. Pro-German faction launches coup in Romania. The coup is put down by General Antonescu who imposes army rule.

⚜ 3. Italian counteroffensive in Albania fails.

⚜ 5. British take 45,000 Italians at Bardia.

⚜ 22. British capture Tobruk in Libya.

BATTLE OF BEDA FROMM   LEND-LEASE ACT

WESTERN FRONT

♠ 9. German long range Condor bombers attack Atlantic convoy and sink 5 ships.

♠ 11. British ships shell Ostend docks.

♠ 12. German cruiser *Admiral Hipper* attacks Atlantic convoy, sinking seven ships.

♠ 22. German battleships *Gneisenau* and *Scharnhorst* attack convoy off Canadian coast, sinking five ships.

⚒ 4. Lofoten Islands Raid. British commandos destroy German weather station and fish-oil factories, and sink six merchant ships.

🤝 11. Britain and USA agree Lend-Lease, an arrangement by which Britain can acquire weapons from the USA on credit.

⚒ 13. Heavy German raids on Glasgow leave 35,000 homeless and 460 dead.

♠ 22. German warships *Gneisenau* and *Scharnhorst* return after sinking 22 ships.

♠ 29. US government impounds all German ships in retaliation for American ships sunk.

EASTERN FRONT

THE MED AND MIDDLE EAST

🤝 1. Bulgaria signs military alliance with Germany and Italy.

REST OF THE WORLD

⚒ 5. Battle of Beda Fomm. British surround and capture 100,000 Italians. Benghazi falls two days later.

⚒ 25. British conquer Italian Somaliland.

⚒ 5. British troops land in Greece.

⚒ 24. German Afrika Korps opens attack in North Africa, capturing El Agheila.

⬧ 27. Anti-German coup in Yugoslavia.

YUGOSLAVIA SURRENDERS   *BISMARCK*

WESTERN FRONT

🔨 2. Germans test world's first jet fighter, the Heinkel 280.

💥 9. British RAF launches successful night raid on Berlin.

🤝 10. Greenland (part of Denmark) puts itself under USA protection.

💥 15. Germans launch heavy night raid on Belfast, killing 500 people.

💥 21. Germans begin five consecutive night raids on Plymouth that destroy the town centre, kill 750 and make 30,000 homeless.

💥 1. Germans begin eight nights of raids on Liverpool that kill 1450, leave 76,000 homeless and destroy much of the docks area.

🔨 5. British recover secret radio-navigation equipment from German bomber.

💥 10. Heaviest night raid on London.

🤝 10. Deputy leader of Germany, Rudolf Hess, flies to Scotland on mysterious mission.

⚓ 18. German battleship *Bismarck* puts to sea to attack British convoys in the Atlantic.

⚓ 27. German battleship *Bismarck* sunk by British warships.

EASTERN FRONT

🤝 13. Russia and Japan sign a five year non-aggression treaty. The treaty does nothing to solve territorial disputes between the two countries, but merely defers them.

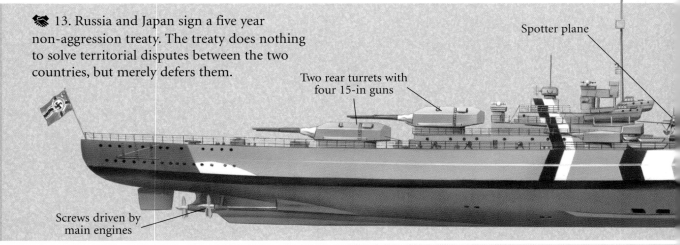

Spotter plane

Two rear turrets with four 15-in guns

Screws driven by main engines

THE MED AND MIDDLE EAST

🤝 23. Russia makes official diplomatic protest to Germany about reconnaissance flights by German aircraft over the Russian border.

🤝 24. Hitler meets with Hungarian leader, Admiral Horthy, who agrees to join the war.

▲ Bismarck *was the sister-ship of* Tirpitz, *and one-to-one more than a match for most British warships. In the end,* Bismarck *was outnumbered.*

REST OF THE WORLD

💥 6. Germany, Italy and Bulgaria invade Yugoslavia and Greece.

🤝 17. Yugoslavia surrenders to Germany.

🤝 22. Greece surrenders to Germany.

💥 3. Italians in Ethiopia defeated by British.

💥 16. Rommel's advance in North Africa reaches Sollum. British in Tobruk under siege.

💥 20. German airborne invasion of Crete.

GERMANY, ITALY, ROMANIA, FINLAND AND HUNGARY INVADE RUSSIA

⚹ 1. Germans accidentally bomb neutral Dublin while trying to find Bristol.

⚹ 11. Germans drop propaganda leaflets across Britain boasting of U-boat success against merchant ships and threatening to starve Britain into surrender.

🤝 14. USA freezes assets of Germany, Italy, Hungary, Romania and Bulgaria and expels German diplomats.

⚹ 31. British RAF launches low-level daylight raid on German ships in Bremen harbour.

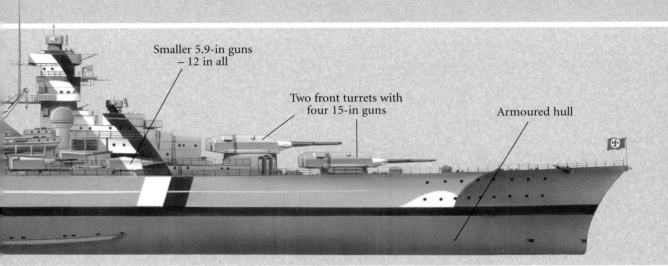

Smaller 5.9-in guns – 12 in all

Two front turrets with four 15-in guns

Armoured hull

🤝 22. Germany, Italy and Romania declare war on Russia and invade with a joint army of 3.2 million men and 3300 tanks.

🤝 26. Finland declares war on Russia.

🤝 27. Hungary declares war on Russia.

⚹ 8. British and Free French invade Vichy French possessions of Syria and Lebanon.

⚹ 14. Operation Battleaxe. British attempt to relieve Tobruk from siege ends in defeat.

RUSSIANS COLLAPSE

BATTLE FOR UKRAINE

WESTERN FRONT

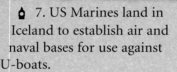

🔥 7. US Marines land in Iceland to establish air and naval bases for use against U-boats.

🤝 19. Germany and Switzerland, now surrounded by Axis states, sign a trade treaty.

◄ *Hermann Goering had such faith in the German air force that he persuaded Hitler that the* Luftwaffe *could defeat Britain on its own.*

🔥 1. Nazi chief Herman Goering issues orders for 'the final solution of the Jewish question' – the extermination of all Jews.

🤝 12. Britain and USA sign the Atlantic Charter, a statement of war aims.

⚓ 21. First convoy carries US weapons to Russia round the north of Norway.

EASTERN FRONT

🤝 28. Dutch government in exile instructs authorities in the Dutch East Indies to halt all oil exports. The move is supported by the USA and is aimed primarily at Japan, which imports most of its oil from this source. It is hoped that a lack of oil will hamper the Japanese war effort in China.

🤝 30. US warships in the Pacific begin boarding Japanese fishing boats, several of which are found to be carrying a naval intelligence officer.

💥 6. Japanese begin series of 40 air raids on Chungking in China.

🤝 25. Japan protests to Russia about passage of merchant ships carrying weapons to Vladivostok through waters claimed by Japan. Russia rejects the protest on the grounds that it claims the waters for its own.

THE MED AND MIDDLE EAST

💥 1. German columns reach rivers Berezina and Dvina as Russians collapse.

💥 15. Germans surround and capture 300,000 Russians at Smolensk.

💥 21. First of 73 German air raids on Moscow.

💥 5. Romanians lay siege to Odessa.

🔧 12. Hitler postpones direct drive on Moscow to divert troops to the Ukraine.

💥 25. Finns attack Hango and Viipuri.

💥 28. Germans capture Tallinn, Estonia.

REST OF THE WORLD

🤝 8. Yugoslavia is divided between Italy, Hungary and newly independent Croatia.

🤝 14. Vichy French forces in Syria and Lebanon surrender to Free French.

💥 24. British ships begin extensive mining of Italian waters.

💥 25. Joint British–Russian occupation of Iran takes place to safeguard oil supplies.

SIEGE OF LENINGRAD

BATTLE OF VYASMA

♣ 4. *Greer* Incident. US destroyer *Greer* attacked by German U-boat U-652 off Iceland. Neither vessel is damaged.

♣ 17. US warships take up convoy escort duties between Canada and Iceland.

☬ 29. Major British air raid on rail works at Amiens is met by formidable new German fighter, the FW190.

♣ 12. German E-boats, fast torpedo boats, sink two British merchant ships within sight of Cromer, Norfolk.

♣ 22. German U-boats sink a British destroyer and fuel tanker during convoy battles.

⚱ 25. Germans shoot 100 Frenchmen at Bordeaux in reprisal for French Resistance shooting of two Germans.

▲ *A U-boat had torpedo tubes at the front and rear, and one deck gun for use when surfaced.*

♣ 10. New Zealand warships, previously serving as part of the British Royal Navy, now reorganized as the Royal New Zealand Navy.

♣ 12. Japanese navy begins a series of extensive naval exercises in the Pacific.

🕵 16. Japanese arrest Richard Sorge, a Russian spy working in Tokyo. They execute him one month later.

⚱ 18. New Japanese government takes office. It is led by General Tojo who is known for his hard-line attitude to China and to relations with the USA and Britain.

☬ 8. Siege of Leningrad begins. Russia's second city surrounded by Axis forces.

☬ 15. Battle of Kiev. Germans surround four Russian armies and take 600,000 prisoners.

☬ 27. Germans reach industrial Donets area.

☬ 1. Operation Typhoon. Germans begin drive to capture Moscow.

☬ 6. Germans encircle and destroy six Russian armies at Vyasma.

☬ 23. Germans capture Kharkov.

♣ 27. Italian torpedo bombers severely damage British battleship HMS *Nelson*.

♣ 2. The British lay a minefield that temporarily closes Piraeus, the main port of Greece.

♣ 25. German bombers sink British cruiser HMS *Latona*.

GERMAN ASSAULT ON MOSCOW HALTED

WESTERN FRONT

⚔ 7. The British launch raid on Berlin, losing 12 percent of aircraft due to bad weather and poor planning. When he learns the facts of the disaster, Churchill sacks head of RAF Bomber Command. The new commander is Arthur 'Bomber' Harris.

⚓ 22. British cruiser HMS *Devonshire* sinks German raider *Atlantis* off Ascension Island.

⚓ 24. British cruiser HMS *Dunedin* sunk by German U-boat U-124.

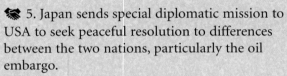

▶ *Japanese planes attacked Pearl Harbor, Hawaii, taking US defences by surprise. There was no declaration of war.*

EASTERN FRONT

🤝 5. Japan sends special diplomatic mission to USA to seek peaceful resolution to differences between the two nations, particularly the oil embargo.

🤝 14. USA agrees to withdraw US Marines from Peking and Shanghai at the request of Japan.

⚓ 19. Battle of Shark Bay, Australia. German raider *Kormorant* and Australian cruiser *Sydney* sink each other.

🤝 20. Japanese diplomatic mission to USA demands immediate resolution or threatens to break off talks.

⚒ 24. US Government instructs all US merchant ships in Pacific to stay in port unless steaming convoy escorted by US Navy warships.

⚓ 26. Large Japanese fleet leaves Japan for secret destination with sealed orders. It is heading for US naval base of Pearl Harbor.

THE MED AND MIDDLE EAST

⚔ 3. Germans capture Kursk.

🏠 6. Stalin makes key speech calling for defence of Russia.

⚔ 9. Germans capture Yalta.

⚔ 14. Romanian–German attack on Sebastopol.

⚔ 24. Germans capture Solnechaya, less than 50 km from Moscow.

⚔ 27. Germans halted 30 km from Moscow by heavy snow and lack of supplies.

REST OF THE WORLD

⚓ 14. British aircraft carrier HMS *Ark Royal* sunk off Gibraltar by German U-boat.

⚒ 17. Raid by Colonel Keyes captures Rommel's HQ, but Rommel is not present.

⚔ 18. Operation Crusader. British 8th Army drives back German–Italian army in North Africa and relieves Tobruk.

⚓ 21. Two Italian cruisers sunk by British.

PEARL HARBOR: JAPAN ATTACKS THE USA

5. Britain declares war on Finland, Romania and Hungary.

11. Germany and Italy declare war on USA.

19. US Martlet fighters (built in British service) shoot down two German Condor bombers attacking an Atlantic convoy. The escort carrier is sunk by German U-boat 24 hours later.

22. First Washington Conference. British chiefs of staff meet with US chiefs of staff to decide war strategy and aims.

24. Free French forces occupy Vichy French colonies off the Canadian coast.

Allies lost 1299 merchant ships in 1941.

3. British Force Z of one battleship, one battle-cruiser and four destroyers reaches Singapore.

5. Large Japanese fleet, including troop transports, leaves ports in southern China, heading south.

7. Pearl Harbor. Japanese aircraft launch surprise attack on US naval base at Pearl Harbor in Hawaii. The Japanese sink five US battleships, cripple three more and sink ten other warships as well as destroying 188 aircraft and killing 2403 servicemen. The Japanese lose 29 aircraft.

7. Japanese invade Malaya.

7. Japan declares war on USA and Britain.

8. Japanese invade the Philippines.

16. Japanese invade Dutch East Indies.

25. Japanese capture Hong Kong.

1. Germans begin panzer attack aimed to surround Moscow.

5. Russians launch surprise counter attack against Germans north of Moscow.

13. Russians begin general offensive on Germans around Moscow.

17. Hitler issues 'Halt Order' forbidding any retreat in face of the Russian attack.

27. Russians recapture Kaluga.

14. British torpedo and damage Italian battleship *Vittorio Veneto* off Sicily.

15. German U-boat U-557 sinks British cruiser HMS *Galatea* off Egypt.

18. British lose one battleship, two cruisers and one destroyer to Italian mini submarines.

25. British 8th Army captures Benghazi and continues drive west along the coast.

1942

The Axis Powers sweep all before them and seem poised for victory.

U-BOAT WARFARE

⚓ 9. German submarines mine the Thames, sinking British destroyer HMS *Vimiera*.

⚓ 11. Operation Drumbeat. German U-boats begin operating in US coastal waters, sinking large numbers of merchant ships steaming singly rather than in convoys.

⚑ 20. German SS chief Reinhard Heydrich organizes the Wansee Conference to prepare for mass extermination of Jews, gypsies and other races deemed to be 'undesirable'.

☀ 2. Japanese capture Manila, capital of the Philippines. Filipino and US forces now under siege in Corregidor and Bataan.

☀ 7. Battle of Changsha sees Japanese attack halted by Chinese.

☀ 8. Japanese land on Borneo.

☀ 10. Japanese begin ten-day assault on Filipino and US forces on Bataan Peninsula.

☀ 15. Japanese capture Kuala Lumpur.

☀ 20. Japanese invade Burma.

☀ 9. Russians begin 12-day assault that drives 100 km into German lines west of Moscow.

⚑ 22. 500,000 evacuated from Leningrad.

☀ 23. Russians break through German lines near Smolensk and surge forwards.

☀ 17. British capture Halfaya Pass.

☀ 29. Surprise counter attack by German–Italians under Rommel recaptures Benghazi and begins British retreat.

FALL OF SINGAPORE HUMILIATES BRITAIN

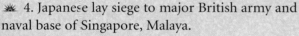 1. King Koadio of Ivory Coast declares for Free French and ousts Vichy French officials.

♠ 12. The Channel Dash. German battleships *Gneisenau*, *Scharnhorst* and cruiser *Prinz Eugen* race up the English Channel to safety in Germany. The British are caught by surprise and fail to stop the ships.

♠ 28. Operation Drumbeat. Germans announce their U-boats have sunk 69 ships in US waters during February.

▼ *A Commando in full kit, ready for combat. When landed in enemy territory, Commandos faced extra danger because Hitler ordered all Commando prisoners to be shot. Some were, although most German army officers ignored Hitler's order.*

✷ 4. Japanese lay siege to major British army and naval base of Singapore, Malaya.

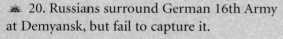 5. Thailand declares war on USA.

✷ 15. Japanese capture Singapore, along with 80,000 British and Empire prisoners.

✷ 19. Japanese aircraft from Dutch East Indies bomb Darwin, northern Australia. Dozens of other raids follow.

✷ 21. British begin retreat from Burma.

✷ 24. US carrier aircraft raid Wake Island.

✷ 20. Russians surround German 16th Army at Demyansk, but fail to capture it.

✷ 23. Russians reach the river Dneiper, but fail to break German resistance.

✷ 5. Rommel's offensive halts at Gazala.

🕵 6. Suitcase bomb explodes in Spanish Morocco. Local newspaper blames British, leading to widespread anti-British rioting.

KEY 🤝 DIPLOMACY 🏠 HOME ♠ NAVAL 🕵 SECRET WAR ✷ BATTLE

JAPANESE VICTORIES IN THE EAST INDIES

WESTERN FRONT

♠ 25. Italian submarine *Pietro Calvi* sinks five merchant ships off Brazil.

♠ 27. St Nazaire Raid. British commando raid destroys dock and harbour gates being used by German naval craft.

⚝ 28. RAF bombers strike the German port of Lübeck. The medieval wooden city centre is destroyed by fire.

♠ 29. Convoy PQ13 is attacked by German U-boats, destroyers and bombers off Norway. The Germans sink five merchant ships and cripple the cruiser HMS *Trinidad*.

EASTERN FRONT

♠ 1. Scattered naval battles around Java result in loss of nine Allied warships and 13 merchant ships. Japanese suffer no losses.

⌂ 3. Americans intern 110,000 Americans of Japanese ancestry.

⚝ 8. Japanese capture Rangoon, Burma.

⚝ 9. Japanese capture Java.

THE MED AND MIDDLE EAST

▲ *Japanese troops celebrate their victory at Bataan in April 1942. Japanese officers wave their swords, in medieval samurai fashion.*

🤝 19. Romanian government claims Transylvania from Hungary. Hitler is forced to intervene to solve dispute between his allies.

🕭 30. Germans estimate ten million Russian casualties in the war so far.

REST OF THE WORLD

⚝ 1. Massive air raids on Malta by Italians.

🤝 13. British allow grain ships to reach Greece.

♠ 22. Battle of Sirte. Both Italians and British take heavy losses.

KEY 🤝 DIPLOMACY ⌂ HOME ♠ NAVAL 🕭 SECRET WAR ⚝ BATTLE

DOOLITTLE RAID ON TOKYO

6. German government cuts food rations.

8. German agents land on Iceland to spy on US military bases.

15. French Resistance attack German army HQ in Arras with grenades.

17. Anti-Vichy French General Henri Giraud escapes from prison camp in Germany and reaches Switzerland.

4. Heavy Japanese air raid on Mandalay in Burma destroys town centre and rail yards.

5. Japanese carrier aircraft attack Colombo in Ceylon, sinking British cruisers and 19 merchant ships.

9. Japanese capture fortified Bataan Peninsula on the Philippines with 70,000 prisoners, and begin attacks on Corregidor.

18. Doolittle Raid. US carrier aircraft bomb Tokyo and four other Japanese cities.

11. Entire Bulgarian government resigns in protest at German demands for troops to fight in Russia.

▶ *A B-25 bomber gets airborne from* USS Hornet, *on its way to bomb Tokyo in the Doolittle Raid of April 1942.*

1. Germans begin 11-day bombing attacks on Malta, causing heavy damage.

7. Exchange of wounded prisoners arranged in Turkey.

WESTERN FRONT

EASTERN FRONT

THE MED AND MIDDLE EAST

REST OF THE WORLD

GERMANS ADVANCE IN RUSSIA

THE BATTLE OF MIDWAY

WESTERN FRONT

☀ 3. Heavy German air raid on Exeter badly damages cathedral and city centre.

⚓ 13. US introduce escorted convoys for merchant ships in Atlantic coastal waters.

⚓ 20. German U-boats sink second Mexican merchant ship in ten days. Mexico issues serious protest to Germany.

🤝 22. Mexico declares war on Germany.

☀ 30. RAF launches 1000 bomber raid on Cologne. City centre is destroyed but the historic cathedral survives.

☀ 1. RAF launches 1000 bomber raid on Essen. Bad weather hampers bomb aiming.

☀ 25. RAF launches 1000 bomber raid on Bremen. Using new Gee radar navigation system, the attacks destroy the business area.

⚓ 26. Germany announces a U-boat blockade of US east coast and lays mines, but it is a ruse to cover a withdrawal of U-boats from the area.

EASTERN FRONT

☀ 2. Japanese capture Mandalay.

⚓ 3. Battle of the Coral Sea. US carrier fleet intercept Japanese fleet heading for New Guinea. Both sides lose an aircraft carrier and the Japanese abandon invasion.

☀ 4. British invade Vichy Madagascar.

☀ 6. Japanese capture Corregidor, the final US outpost on the Philippines.

🐛 14. American code-breakers intercept Japanese signals about invasion of Midway.

⚓ 4. Battle of Midway. Complex battle lasting three days ends with the Japanese losing four carriers and two cruisers, and the US losing one carrier. The naval advantage in the Pacific now lies with the Americans.

THE MED AND MIDDLE EAST

☀ 9. Battle of Kharkhov begins with Russian attack, followed by German counter attack. After six weeks the battle ends inconclusively.

☀ 23. Sudden panzer attack at Barvenkovo captures 250,000 Russians.

☀ 1. Germans begin siege of Sebastopol.

☀ 27. Germans launch major offensive in the Ukraine aimed at capturing Stalingrad and the Caucuses oil fields. Over 100 divisions smash Russian lines.

REST OF THE WORLD

⚓ 11. Three British destroyers sunk by German bombers off Egyptian coast.

☀ 26. Rommel launches Italian–German attack on British at Gazala.

⚓ 12. British convoys to Malta take heavy losses. Malta is dangerously short of supplies.

☀ 17. Rommel breaks British defences at Gazala and on 21 June captures Tobruk.

CONVOY PQ17

STALINGRAD ATTACKED

⚓ 4. British convoy PQ17 is ordered to scatter after German battleship *Tirpitz* approaches. The merchant ships are then picked off by U-boats and bombers – 24 of 38 ships are sunk.

⚓ 10. German U-boats begin new campaign in the Caribbean.

✵ 11. RAF bombs U-boat yards at Danzig.

✵ 15. RAF Spitfires carry out low-level raids on northern France. Over 200 aircraft take part.

✈ 18. First test flight of the German Me262 jet fighter.

🤝 13. Brazil declares war on Germany and Italy after U-boats sink Brazilian ships.

✵ 17. First all-American bombing raid in Europe takes place as 12 B-17 Flying Fortresses attack rail yards at Rouen.

✵ 19. The Dieppe Raid. Canadian and British forces land around Dieppe to test amphibious assault tactics. The raid ends in disaster with 60 percent casualties and no gains.

⚑ 31. Police in Ulster arrest 90 IRA men planning attack on US troops stationed in Northern Ireland.

⚓ 13. Japanese submarines begin five-week campaign off the southeast coast of Australia.

✵ 21. Japanese invade New Guinea at Buna and begin overland march to Port Moresby.

✵ 30. Chinese capture Tsingtien.

◀ *The Flying Fortress was aptly named – the B-17 bristled with guns. B-17s flew by day, in tight formation, while Lancasters normally bombed at night.*

✵ 7. US Marines land on Guadalcanal in the Solomon Islands.

⚓ 8. In the Battle of Savo in the Solomons the Allies lose four cruisers and the Japanese one. US Marines on Guadalcanal are now cut off.

✵ 21. US Marines on Guadalcanal drive off strong Japanese landing forces.

⚓ 24. In the Battle of the Eastern Solomons, the Japanese lose one carrier and one US carrier is badly damaged.

✵ 3. Germans capture Sebastopol.

✵ 5. Germans reach the river Don.

✵ 17. Germans gain control of the Donets coal field.

✵ 25. Germans cross the river Don.

✵ 19. German assault on Stalingrad is begun by the 6th Army under Paulus.

✵ 23. German air raid on Stalingrad kills 40,000 and destroys city centre.

✵ 25. Germans reach Mozduck, Cauccasus.

✵ 1. Rommel's advance of 650 km in 35 days into Egypt is halted by the British 8th Army at the five-day First Battle of El Alamein.

⚓ 7. The British Pedestal convoy leaves Gibraltar with 14 merchant ships. Only four ships reach Malta, the escort having lost one carrier, two cruisers and one destroyer.

LIBERTY SHIPS

BATTLE OF EL ALAMEIN

WESTERN FRONT

⚜ 4. German bomber attacking Torquay is shot down, crashlanding on the beach.

♠ 23. First of many hundreds of prefabricated 'Liberty Ship' merchant vessels launched in the USA just 10 days after construction began.

⚜ 25. RAF launch precision, low-level raid on Gestapo HQ in central Oslo, Norway.

⚜ 29. German bomber hits a school in Sussex, killing 31 children and injuring 28.

⚓ 3. First test launch of German V-2 rocket.

⚜ 4. Successful British commando raid on Sark, in the occupied Channel Islands.

♠ 7. German U-boat pack sent to South Africa, where it will sink 28 ships in three weeks.

⚜ 31. German daylight bomber raid on Canterbury carried out at low level to avoid defences. Heavy damage is caused and ten attackers shot down.

EASTERN FRONT

⚜ 5. Major Japanese reinforcements land on Guadalcanal.

⚜ 11. Japanese advance on Port Moresby halted by Australian troops on Kakoda Trail.

⚜ 13. Japanese attack on US Marines on Guadalcanal defeated on 'Bloody Ridge'.

⚜ 21. British attack at Arakan in Burma begins well, but ends in failure.

♠ 11. US warships sink a Japanese cruiser in Battle of Cape Esperance, Guadalcanal.

♠ 13. Japanese battleships shell US Marines on Guadalcanal on the first of three consecutive nights.

🤝 17. US agrees to arm 30 Chinese divisions.

⚜ 23. Japanese launch four-day assault on US positions on Guadalcanal. Attack fails.

♠ 26. Battle of Santa Cruz end with sinking of a US carrier and a Japanese cruiser.

THE MED AND MIDDLE EAST

⚜ 4. Germans reach river Volga south of Stalingrad, cutting off Russian defenders.

⚜ 13. Germans begin major assault on central Stalingrad.

⚜ 24. Germans reach Volga in Stalingrad.

⚜ 14. Germans begin new 14-day attack in Stalingrad, capturing key tractor factory.

REST OF THE WORLD

⚜ 4. Battle of Alam Halfa ends with the failure of a German attack on the British positions at El Alamein.

⚜ 14. British raid on Tobruk defeated.

⚜ 20. Italian bombers heading for Gibraltar bomb Spain by mistake.

⚜ 23. Second Battle of El Alamein opens with attack by British and Australians.

STALINGRAD ATTACKED

GUADALCANAL

11. German and Italian forces occupy Vichy France. Military rule imposed throughout France. Italians seize Corsica.

15. Church bells rung throughout Britain to celebrate victory at El Alamein.

27. Vichy French Admiral de Laborde orders the scuttling of all French warships to prevent them being seized by Germans. A total of 56 ships are sunk, including two battle-cruisers, one battleship and seven cruisers.

▶ *General Charles de Gaulle led the Free French Forces from exile in London. He had a prickly relationship with the British government, which tended to keep secrets from him.*

2. US scientist Enrico Fermi achieves the first controlled nuclear chain reaction.

11. British commandos paddle canoes up river Gironde to sink six ships in Bordeaux.

28. Free French leader General de Gaulle joins with General Giraud in appeal for unity between Free French and ex-Vichy French.

31. Battle of the Barents Sea. German warships *Lützow* and *Admiral Hipper* fail to sink helpless convoy due to poor leadership.

♣ Allies lost 1570 merchant ships in 1942.

1. US Marines counter attack Japanese on Guadalcanal, driving off attackers.

5. Final surrender of Vichy French forces on Madagascar to British and Free French.

12. Night action off Guadalcanal sees Japanese lose one battleship and US one cruiser. The following night a second Japanese battleship is sunk.

30. Night action off Guadalcanal ends in confusion and defeat for US cruisers.

1. Australians capture Gona on New Guinea as they drive the Japanese back.

7. US attack on Guadalcanal timed to mark anniversary of Pearl Harbor.

20. Japanese bomb Calcutta at night.

21. Australian tanks breach Japanese defences at Buna, New Guinea.

11. German assault engineers launch failed bid to crush Russians in Stalingrad.

19. Russians launch pincer attack with 11 armies to surround Germans in Stalingrad.

25. Germans air supply men in Stalingrad.

12. Operation Winter Storm. German attempt to relieve troops trapped in Stalingrad begins, but fails after five days.

23. Renewed German drive to reach Stalingrad halted by Russians at Myshkova.

2. Second Battle of El Alamein ends in victory for British under General Montgomery.

8. Operation Torch. US, British and Free French troops land in Vichy-controlled Algeria.

1. Ethiopia declares war on Germany.

6. German attack at Medjez is defeated.

13. Germans retreat from El Agheila.

1943

The Netherlands declares that it will remain neutral in any war.

CASABLANCA CONFERENCE

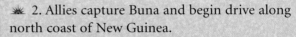

🤝 15. Churchill and Roosevelt meet in the Casablanca Conference to decide on war aims for the coming year. They give top priority to defeating the U-boats and agree Sicily is to be invaded in the summer of 1943.

🎗 20. Germans launch low-level attack on London docks, causing heavy damage.

🎗 2. Allies capture Buna and begin drive along north coast of New Guinea.

🎗 6. Battle of Huon Gulf. Massed Allied air attacks destroy Japanese troop convoy heading for New Guinea.

🎗 17. British launch a second assault into the Arakan region of Burma. As before, the attack begins well, but later fails in the face of Japanese counter attacks.

🎗 10. Russians begin attacks on German 6th Army trapped in and around Stalingrad.

🎗 13. Russians begin drive south from Kharkhov to cut off German forces in the Caucasus, but are halted and driven back.

🎗 19. British 8th Army captures Homs.

🎗 20. German attack at Ousseltia driven off by Free French.

🎗 23. British 8th Army captures Tripoli.

MASSED GERMAN SURRENDER AT STALINGRAD

♠ 7. Atlantic convoy SC118 attacked by German U-boats and six ships sunk.

♠ 16. Students riot in Munich after local Nazi leader makes insulting speech. Two students are later executed as traitors.

♣ 18. Test flight of new US B29 Superfortress bomber ends in disastrous crash that kills engineers and chief test pilot.

♠ 25. German U-boats begin five-day attack on convoy ON166, sinking 15 ships.

▲ *US President Roosevelt and British Prime Minister Churchill discuss events at Casablanca, January 1943.*

♠ 1. Japanese destroyers begin night-time evacuation of surviving troops on Guadalcanal. By 8 February the Americans have total control of the island.

⚔ 14. British begin first Chindit operation as self-supporting columns penetrate Japanese lines in Burma.

⚔ 2. Battle of Stalingrad ends with surrender of German Field Marshal von Paulus and 100,000 survivors of his 6th Army.

⚔ 8. Russians recapture Kursk.

⚔ 4. British 8th Army enters Tunisia.

⚔ 4. British 8th Army takes Medenine.

⚔ 13. Surprise German attack at Battle of Kasserine Pass disrupts Allied advance.

BATTLE OF THE RUHR   KATYN FOREST

WESTERN FRONT

⚜ 5. British RAF opens 'Battle of the Ruhr', a sustained campaign of night bombing aimed at destroying German industrial output in the key Ruhr Valley. The campaign lasts until June.

⚓ 6. The largest convoy battle of the war rages for six days around convoys HX228 and HX229. The Allies lose 21 ships while the Germans lose four U-boats.

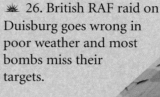

🤝 7. Bolivia declares war on Germany, Italy and Japan.

⚜ 26. British RAF raid on Duisburg goes wrong in poor weather and most bombs miss their targets.

▲ *The Lancaster was one of the main Allied weapons of the war. The bomb-aimer peered through the glass 'bubble' on the underside of the aircraft's nose.*

EASTERN FRONT

⚓ 2. Battle of the Bismarck Sea. Allied aircraft and surface ships destroy large Japanese convoy and escort off New Guinea.

⚜ 13. Chinese begin moderately successful offensive in the Yangtse Valley.

⚜ 7. Japanese launch massive air strikes on Allied shipping in the Solomons. Two warships and three transports are sunk.

⚜ 18. Japanese naval commander in chief Admiral Yamamoto is killed when his transport aircraft is shot down by US fighters over Bougainville.

THE MED AND MIDDLE EAST

🏠 2. Mussolini withdraws all Italian troops from the Eastern Front.

⚜ 12. Russians capture Vyazma.

🤝 31. Hitler meets King Boris of Bulgaria, but fails to persuade him to join war on Russia.

🏠 12. Germans announce discovery of mass graves of Polish officers murdered in 1940 by Russians in the Katyn Forest.

🏠 19. Jews launch abortive uprising in Warsaw Ghetto. Fighting ends after 27 days.

REST OF THE WORLD

🏠 9. German Erwin Rommel gives up command in North Africa due to ill health.

⚜ 28. British 8th Army capture German–Italian defences at Mareth.

⚜ 6. Battle of Wadi Akarit. British 8th Army break German outer defences.

⚜ 8. British 8th Army captures port of Sfax.

⚓ 16. British destroyer sunk off Sicily.

SURRENDER OF TUNIS   OPERATION CARTWHEEL

WESTERN FRONT

⚜ 3. German bombers lay extensive minefields off the English east coast.

♣ 11. Battle around convoy HX237 results in three U-boats sunk for no British loss.

⚜ 16. The Dambusters Raid. Elite force of 19 RAF Lancasters bomb the dams that supply water to the Ruhr industrial belt. Two dams are destroyed, one damaged.

♣ 23. Renewed attacks by German U-boats result in nine U-boats sunk, only one ship lost.

♣ 24. Germany suspends U-boat attacks.

⚜ 14. Operation Musketry. RAF Coastal Command begin series of daily patrols over Bay of Biscay to find and sink German U-boats before they reach the shipping lanes.

⚜ 20. First Allied 'shuttle' raid. A force of RAF Lancaster bombers bomb Germany, and then fly on to Algiers. They are refuelled and rearmed to bomb Italy on their return to Britain.

EASTERN FRONT

⚜ 4. Japanese counter offensive in the Chinese Yangtse Valley begins.

⚜ 7. Australians capture Mubo, New Guinea.

⚜ 20. Japanese counter offensive in the Yangtse Valley halted by determined Chinese resistance.

⚜ 30. End of Japanese resistance on occupied Attu Island in the Aleutian Islands off Alaska, the only US territory to be occupied during the course of the war.

♣ 8. Japanese battleship *Mutsu* mysteriously explodes in Hiroshima harbour.

♣ 16. German raider *Michel* begins attacking ships west of Australia.

⚜ 16. Of 94 Japanese aircraft raiding Guadalcanal, 93 are shot down.

⚜ 30. Americans begin Operation Cartwheel – a complex series of naval and amphibious operations to isolate major Japanese base on Rabaul.

THE MED AND MIDDLE EAST

⚜ 1. Russians begin extended series of bombing raids on rail junctions and yards behind German lines in Russia.

REST OF THE WORLD

⚜ 6. Massive Allied attack strikes German-Italian defences around Tunis.

⚜ 12. Surrender of German-Italian forces at Tunis. There are no Axis forces left in Africa.

⚜ 11. Italian island of Pantellaria surrenders after ten-day bombardment.

⚜ 12. Italian island of Lampedusa surrenders to RAF pilot who crash lands.

HAMBURG FIRESTORM

PEENEMUNDE RAID

WESTERN FRONT

⚜ 24. Operation Gomorrah. Sustained heavy RAF raids on Hamburg lasting four nights result in horrific firestorm, killing 42,000, injuring 37,000 and destroying 600 factories. Nazi propaganda chief reviews the destruction and reports to Hitler that Germany could lose the war if such raids continue.

⚒ 24. First test flight of British jet fighter, the Gloster Meteor.

🤝 14. 1st Quebec Conference. Churchill and Roosevelt agree to launch joint invasion of France in summer 1944.

⚜ 17. The Peenemunde Raid. RAF bombers launch night raid on German weapons development works at Peenemunde.

⚜ 17. First Schweinfurt Raid. US bombers launch daylight raid on heavily defended ball bearing factory at Schweinfurt. 60 out of 230 aircraft are shot down.

🏠 28. Germans impose martial law on Denmark after civilian government resigns.

EASTERN FRONT

♠ 12. Battle of Kolombangara. Japanese lose cruiser *Jintsu* while US ships *Honolulu*, *St Louis* and *Gwin* are badly damaged.

⚜ 16. Australians capture Mount Tambu, New Guinea.

♠ 27. US battleships *Mississippi* and *Idaho* fight one-sided battle with non-existent Japanese fleet due to malfunction of radar on the Mississippi. Event becomes known as Battle of the Pips.

♠ 6. In the Battle of Vella Gulf, US destroyers ambush and sink two of four Japanese destroyers.

⚜ 17. American carrier aircraft carry out heavy raids on Japanese positions at Wewak, New Guinea.

THE MED AND MIDDLE EAST

⚜ 5. Battle of Kursk opens with massive German attacks north and south of Kursk.

⚜ 12. German attacks at Kursk halted in largest tank battle in history, south of Kursk.

⚜ 15. Russian counter attack takes Orel.

⚜ 5. Russians capture Belgorod.

⚜ 13. Russians launch major offensive near Smolensk.

⚜ 23. Russians recapture Kharkhov.

⚜ 26. Russians launch offensive in Ukraine.

REST OF THE WORLD

⚜ 10. Joint US–British invasion of Sicily begins.

⚜ 22. Americans capture Palermo, Sicily.

🏠 25. Italian dictator Mussolini is sacked and arrested on orders of King Victor Emmanuel.

🤝 2. Italian ambassador in Portugal asks British ambassador for surrender terms.

⚜ 17. British and Americans complete occupation of Sicily with capture of Messina.

ITALY SURRENDERS

RUSSIANS ADVANCE

♠ 14. Germans finish equipping their U-boats with anti-aircraft guns and acoustic torpedoes. U-boats are sent back to the Atlantic to attack convoys.

♠ 19. German U-boats attack convoy ON202, sinking seven ships for loss of three U-boats.

♠ 20. British mini submarines disable German battleship *Tirpitz* in Alta Fjord, Norway.

⚔ 14. Second Schweinfurt Raid. 60 out of 290 US bombers are shot down. US 8th Air Force temporarily abandons daylight raids over Germany.

♠ 17. British naval ships land Free Norwegian troops to liberate Norwegian Spitzbergen Island.

⚑ 28. In USA, 530,000 coalminers go on strike over pay. President Roosevelt declares martial law in mining areas. Strike collapses after one week.

⚔ 15. Lae, New Guinea, captured by Allies.

♠ 18. US carrier aircraft attack Japanese positions on Tarawa in the Gilbert Islands.

♠ 23. US submarine *Trigger* sinks Japanese convoy of oil tankers off Formosa.

♠ 26. Japanese begin evacuation of the Solomon Islands.

⚔ 3. Australians take Finschhafen, New Guinea.

⚔ 6. Japanese evacuate Vella Lavella, sinking two US destroyers that try to intervene.

⚔ 11. Japanese aircraft bomb Madras.

⚓ 20. Japanese carriers transport aircraft to Rabaul to prepare for offensive in Solomons.

🤝 21. Japan grants independence to puppet government in the Philippines.

⚑ 25. Burma railway completed.

⚔ 13. Russians launch offensive north of Smolensk.

⚔ 15. Russians break through at Desna.

⚔ 17. Russians capture Bryansk.

⚔ 22. Russians cross river Dnieper at Kiev.

⚔ 13. Russians capture Zaporozhe.

⚔ 30. Russians cross the Dnieper.

⚔ 30. Russians cut off German forces in the Crimea.

🤝 8. Italian surrender announced.

⚔ 9. Allies invade Italy at Salerno.

⚔ 9. Germans seize all strategic points in Italy and forcibly disarm Italian forces.

⚔ 1. Allied 5th Army enters Naples.

⚔ 3. Germans seize Italian bases in Greece.

🤝 13. Italy declares war on Germany.

US LOSES HEAVILY AS THEY CAPTURE TARAWA ISLAND

▲ *The Pacific battles took a heavy toll of US army and marines. These marines were photographed on Bougainville Island in 1944. Many of their comrades were dead or wounded.*

WESTERN FRONT

♣ 3. German E-boats sink three ships off Hastings.

♣ 15. Germans abandon U-boat campaign in the Atlantic.

⚔ 18. Battle of Berlin. British RAF begins five-month-long campaign of night bombing of the German capital that kills 6000 civilians and leaves 1.5 million homeless.

⚔ 21. British and Free Norwegian Commandoes raid Arendal, Norway.

EASTERN FRONT

⚔ 1. Americans land on Bougainville, Solomons. Japanese cruiser Sendai is sunk.

⚔ 11. US aircraft launch raids on Rabaul.

⚔ 20. US Marines land on Tarawa and Betio in the Gilbert Islands. Japanese defenders fight to the death, inflicting heavy casualties.

♣ 25. Battle of Cape St George. American destroyers annihilate Japanese destroyer squadron.

THE MED AND MIDDLE EAST

⚔ 1. Russians land on the Crimea.

⚔ 6. Russians capture Kiev, then cut strategic Odessa–Leningrad railway.

REST OF THE WORLD

⚔ 4. Americans cross the river Volturno.

⚔ 19. British establish bridgehead over Sangro.

⚱ 21. General Kesselring takes over as German commander in Mediterranean.

NAVAL BATTLE OF NORTH CAPE

🤝 4. Second Cairo Conference between Allies gives priority to Pacific campaign not Burma.

🔔 12. Hitler appoints Field Marshal Rommel to command the defence of western Europe.

🔔 24. Commanders chosen for invasion of France. US General Eisenhower – overall command, British General Montgomery – land forces, Air Marshal Tedder – air forces, and Admiral Ramsay – naval forces.

⚓ 26. Battle of North Cape. German battleship *Scharnhorst* sunk off Norway.

⚓ Allies lost 597 merchant ships in 1943.

▼ *General Dwight D Eisenhower, US Army, was appointed to command the invasion of Western Europe. He was a skilful 'man-manager'.*

⚓ 9. American ships attack Nauru and Kwajeilein islands.

🎆 27. Australians capture Pimple Hill, New Guinea.

🎆 14. Russians capture Cherkassy.

🎆 17. German attack at Kirovograd fails.

🔔 19. Russia adopts a new national anthem in place of the Communist Party song.

🔔 22. Spanish fascist volunteers return home.

🎆 6. British 8th Army crosses the river Moro.

🎆 28. Canadians capture Ortona after prolonged street fighting.

1944

The Allied sweep across the Pacific gathers pace as the end nears for Nazi Germany.

LENINGRAD SIEGE ENDS

☀ 4. Germans launch the 'Little Blitz', a series of heavy raids on London and southeast England. There will be 14 night attacks of about 450 aircraft in the following five weeks.

⚰ 5. Outspoken Danish pastor Kaj Munk shot by Germans for anti-German speeches.

🤝 26. Liberia declares war on Germany and Italy.

☀ 10. British capture Maungdaw, Burma.

☀ 11. German wolf pack 'Monsoon' begins operations in Indian Ocean. They will sink 17 ships before returning to Germany in March.

☀ 31. Americans invade Kwajalein and Majuro in the Marshall Islands.

☀ 4. Advancing Russians reach the 1939 Polish border at Olevsk.

☀ 14. Russians launch offensive from Leningrad, finally ending the siege.

☀ 19. Russians capture Novgorod.

⚰ 11. Italian Count Ciano shot by Fascists.

☀ 15. Germans pull back to river Rapido.

☀ 22. Allied landings at Anzio begin well, but fail to move inland rapidly.

ASSAULT ON MONTE CASSINO BEGINS IN ITALY

⚜ 20. American 8th Air Force launches 'Big Week' – seven days of heavy co-ordinated raids on German industrial targets, mostly aircraft factories.

⚜ 22. American bombers lose their way and accidentally bomb Dutch city of Nijmegen, inflicting heavy civilian casualties.

▼ *US troops destroy one of the last Japanese strongholds on tiny Kwajalein Atoll in February 1944. Each island group captured became a base for the Allies' next attack.*

⚓ 3. Americans begin construction of massive dockyard facilities on remote Majuro Island to serve as forward supply base.

⚜ 4. Japanese launch major attack in Arakan area of Burma.

⚓ 10. Japanese fleet abandons forward base at Truk after heavy American bombing.

⚓ 13. Japanese submarine sinks British troopship Khedive Ismail, killing 2000.

⚜ 6. Russians cross river Dnieper at Nikopol.

⚜ 21. Russians capture Krivoi Rog, key iron mining area in the Ukraine.

⚜ 25. Russians launch heavy bombing raid on Helsinki, capital of Finland.

⚜ 15. Allies bomb Monte Cassino, destroying medieval monastery but fail to break through.

⚜ 19. German attack at Anzio is driven off.

THE GREAT ESCAPE

SIEGE OF KOHIMA

WESTERN FRONT

⚔ 6. First major daylight air raid on Berlin carried out by 730 bombers of the US 8th Air Force, protected by 800 new Mustang long-range fighters.

⚓ 13. German U-boat U-852 torpedoes Greek merchant ship *Peleus*, then machine-guns the survivors in their lifeboats. Only three of 35 crew survive.

⚔ 23. RAF 1000 bomber raid on Berlin.

🏠 24. The Great Escape. 76 Allied airmen escape from prison camp Stalag Lufe III. Fifty are recaptured and shot by the Gestapo.

⚔ 11. Precision, low-level raid by RAF Mosquitoes destroys Gestapo HQ in The Hague, Netherlands.

⚔ 13. Allied air forces carry out heavy raids on German coastal defences in France.

⚔ 18. Germans launch last big air raid on London with 125 bombers.

⚔ 19. British bombers drop mines along the river Danube.

🤝 22. Turkey ceases exports of war materials to Germany and its allies.

EASTERN FRONT

⚔ 7. Japanese launch major offensive over the river Chindwin, Burma, towards India.

⚔ 20. Chinese troops occupy the Hukawng Valley, northern Burma.

⚓ 20. American warships bombard Emirau and Kavieng in the Bismarck Archipelago.

⚔ 29. Siege of Imphal. Japanese troops advancing from Burma surround British supply base at Imphal.

⚔ 6. Siege of Kohima. Japanese troops advancing from Burma surround British outpost at Kohima.

🏠 14. Munitions ship Fort Stikine explodes in Bombay harbour, sinking 27 other ships and killing 1500 people.

⚔ 20. Siege of Kohima. British reinforcements arrive at Kohima.

⚔ 22. American forces land at Hollandia and Aitape, New Guinea.

THE MED AND MIDDLE EAST

⚔ 15. Russians reach the river Bug, Ukraine.

🤝 18. Admiral Horthy visits Hitler to ask that Hungarian troops be withdrawn from Russia. Hitler refuses.

⚔ 19. Germany invades Hungary.

⚔ 3. Russian advance reaches Romania.

⚔ 10. Russians capture Odessa.

🤝 16. Nazi puppet government in Hungary announces that all Jews are to be arrested.

⚔ 16. Russians capture Yalta.

REST OF THE WORLD

⚔ 1. New German attack at Anzio begins, but is driven off after four days.

⚔ 16. New Zealand attack at Cassino makes some gains, but fails to break through.

🏠 4. Free Greek army begins 20-day mutiny against King George in favour of a republic.

ALLIED VICTORY AT MONTE CASSINO IN ITALY

3. Spain agrees to cut exports of metal ores to Germany.

8. 'Oil Offensive' opens with massive American bombing raids on synthetic oil plants in Germany. Lack of oil supplies has been identified as key strategic weakness for German armed forces.

14. Around 90 German bombers raid Bristol.

17. French Resistance destroy ball bearing factory at Ivry-sur-Seine.

18. Pro-German riots break out in Constantinople. Turkish government imposes martial law.

20. Allied bombers begin massed raids on rail junctions and yards in northern France.

26. Serpa Pinto Incident. German U-boat U-541 stops neutral Portuguese liner *Serpa Pinto* as it heads for Canada. Crew and passengers are ordered into lifeboats but U-541 leaves without sinking liner. Crew and passengers reboard ship after nine hours, but three die of exposure.

4. British capture key junction on the Maungdaw-Buthidaung Road, Burma.

6. Siege of Imphal. British launch offensive to break through to Imphal from India.

17. US–Chinese forces capture Myitkyina Airfield, Burma.

19. US attack Marcus and Wake islands.

23. Chinese launch offensive in the Honan Province.

27. US forces land on Biak Island, off north coast of New Guinea.

29. Japanese land reinforcements on Biak.

30. Team of Japanese sabotage agents is landed on Ceylon from submarine, but fail to achieve much damage before they are killed.

▲ *Heinrich Himmler, head of the SS, or Schutzstaffel (Protection Squadron), was in charge of concentration camps and internal security across occupied Europe.*

1. Russian dictator Stalin asks Marshals Zhukov and Vasilevsky to plan final offensive to conquer Germany.

9. Russians capture Sebastopol.

20. German V-2 rocket is captured by Polish Resistance and smuggled into London.

30. German offensive at Jassy, Romania, makes limited gains.

11. Allied 5th and 8th Armies launch attack on Monte Cassino and Gustav Line defences.

18. Free Polish capture key Monastery Hill at Cassino. The Germans retreat.

20. Canadians break through German defences. Germans retreat from Anzio.

D-DAY: ALLIED INVASION OF EUROPE

WESTERN FRONT

⚜ 5. Massive attacks by Allied air forces in Normandy. They target rail lines, bridges and German artillery batteries.

⚜ 6. D-Day. Allied invasion of France. At dawn, five divisions of British, Canadian and US troops are landed on Normandy beaches while Allied warships and bombers pound German defences. Airborne troops have already landed and seized key targets up to 8 km inland.

⚜ 7. Normandy. British reach Bayeux. German resistance stiffens.

⚜ 12. Normandy. Allied beachheads link up to form continuous front.

▲ D-day. US troops wait for the ramp of the landing craft to drop.

EASTERN FRONT

⚓ 11. American carrier aircraft attack various targets in the Marianas Islands.

⚓ 13. American battleships bombard Saipan, Marianas.

⚜ 14. First US air raid by B29 Superfortress bombers strikes Japan. The aircraft fly from bases in China.

⚜ 15. Americans land on Saipan.

⚜ 18. Japanese offensive captures city of Changsha, China.

⚓ 19. Battle of the Philippine Sea. Three-day naval battle sees the Japanese carrier-based air force effectively destroyed by American pilots from carriers in the Philippine Sea.

⚜ 22. Siege of Imphal. British break through to besieged garrison. Japanese start to retreat back to Burma.

⚜ 27. Battle of Hengyang sees Japanese advance halted by the Chinese.

THE MED AND MIDDLE EAST

⚜ 9. Russians launch major offensive against the Finns, north of Leningrad.

⚜ 20. Russians capture Viipuri, Finland.

⚜ 20. Russian partisans begin three-day campaign of sabotage against railways in German-occupied Ukraine.

⚜ 23. Russians launch their largest offensive of the war so far in Byelorussia with 1.2 million men and 5200 tanks. German defences collapse within a few hours.

REST OF THE WORLD

⚓ 1. Last German supply ship reaches Crete. Most island garrisons now isolated.

⚜ 4. Allied 5th Army enters Rome after city is abandoned by German commander Kesselring without fighting so that the ancient monuments would not be damaged.

⚜ 17. British 8th Army captures Assissi.

⚜ 26. South Africans capture Chiusi.

JULY BOMB PLOT   WARSAW UPRISING

WESTERN FRONT

⚔ 8. Normandy. British attack at Caen fails.

⚔ 17. German commander in France, Field Marshal Rommel, is badly wounded by British aircraft. He is taken to hospital in Germany.

🕯 20. July Bomb Plot. Group of German army officers narrowly fail to kill Hitler by planting a bomb in his HQ. Officers in Paris launch coup against Nazis, but this collapses when it is learned that Hitler has survived. Plotters are executed. The Gestapo track down anyone with links to the plot, disrupting German military hierarchy.

⚔ 1. US 1st Army breaks out of Normandy at Avranches, advancing rapidly to south.

⚔ 4. First Allied jet aircraft enters combat – the British Gloster Meteor fighter.

⚔ 11. Americans capture Angers and Nantes.

⚔ 13. Americans capture Orleans.

⚔ 15. Germans pummelled by Allied air forces at Falaise.

🕯 19. Paris Uprising. French Resistance, police and civilians attack German garrison.

⚔ 25. German garrison in Paris surrenders.

EASTERN FRONT

⚔ 7. Americans wipe out Japanese defenders of Saipan.

🕯 18. Tojo resigns as Japanese prime minister due to defeats in the Pacific. He is replaced by equally hardline General Koiso.

⚔ 21. Americans land on Guam.

⚔ 24. Americans land on Tinian.

⚔ 28. Americans complete capture of Biak.

⚔ 30. Americans land at Sansapor, completing occupation of New Guinea.

⚔ 10. Americans secure control of Guam. Isolated groups of Japanese continue guerrilla warfare from the jungle. Final Japanese soldier surrenders in 1972.

⚔ 16. Japanese abandon defensive positions along the Burma–India border and pull back to central Burma.

THE MED AND MIDDLE EAST

⚔ 3. German 4th Army cut off at Minsk.

⚔ 7. Finns retreat to defensive U Line.

⚔ 10. Russians begin major offensive in Baltic States. Germans retreat slowly.

⚔ 11. German 4th Army surrenders.

⚔ 1. Polish Home Army launch Warsaw Uprising. Russians refuse to help.

🤝 23. King Michael of Romania sacks the government and surrenders to Russia.

🤝 25. Romania declares war on Germany.

REST OF THE WORLD

🕯 1. Brazilian Expeditionary Force leaves Brazil to fight in Italy.

⚔ 17. British 8th Army crosses river Arno.

⚔ 15. Allied 7th Army lands near Nice and drives rapidly inland.

⚔ 22. Allied forces in Italy reach Metauro.

⚔ 27. Germans evacuate Athens.

ATTACK ON ARNHEM   BATTLE OF LEYTE GULF

WESTERN FRONT

⚜ 1. Canadians capture Dieppe, British capture Arras. Americans capture Verdun.

⚜ 3. British capture Brussels after advancing 360 km in just four days.

⚜ 8. First German V-2 rocket lands on London, killing three and demolishing several buildings.

⚜ 11. US 1st Army enters Germany near Trier.

⚜ 17. British and Polish paratroops seize key bridge across Rhine at Arnhem. Ground attack fails to reach them and most surrender. Allied offensive in the west is halted.

⚜ 3. RAF bomb Dutch sea dykes, causing extensive flooding behind German lines.

⚜ 7. US 1st Army breaches German Siegfried Line Defences near Aachen, but fails to achieve significant breakthrough.

⚜ 14. 2000 RAF bombers raid Duisburg.

⌂ 14. Rommel commits suicide after being implicated in July Bomb Plot.

◀ *The fighter-bomber version of the twin-engined Me 262 jet was heavier and thus slower, making it less effective in combat than enemy fighter jets.*

EASTERN FRONT

⚜ 15. US forces begin landing on the Palau Islands.

⚜ 16. Japanese carrier Unyo sunk by US submarine Barb off China.

⚜ 12. Battle of Formosa. Allied and Japanese fleets clash, but results are inconclusive.

⚜ 20. Allied forces land on Leyte, Philippines.

⚜ 24. Battle of Leyte Gulf. Four Japanese fleets converge on the Philippines to destroy Allied fleets and landing forces. Confused three-day battle ends in total defeat for Japanese navy, which loses four carriers, three battleships, ten cruisers and 11 destroyers.

THE MED AND MIDDLE EAST

⚜ 2. Russians reach Bulgarian border.

🤝 8. Bulgaria declares war on Germany.

🤝 10. Finland surrenders.

⚜ 22. Russians capture Tallinn, Estonia.

⌂ 2. End of Warsaw Uprising. Polish Home Army destroyed by Germans.

⚜ 4. German Army Group North cut off in Baltic States.

⚜ 13. Russians capture Riga, Latvia.

REST OF THE WORLD

⚜ 24. British land in Greece and begin pursuit of retreating Germans. Naval detachments are sent to occupy Greek islands. Various Greek factions agree temporary unity.

⌂ 30. Agreement between Greek factions breaks down as royalist government in exile bans Communist Party.

KAMIKAZE BEGINS

BATTLE OF THE BULGE

WESTERN FRONT

- 2. Liberation of Belgium completed.
- 5. Allies capture Flushing.
- 7. Franklin D Roosevelt re-elected as US president after hiding true extent of his ill health.
- 8. US 3rd Army begins offensive near Metz.
- 12. German battleship *Tirpitz* sunk in Tromso Fjord, Norway, by RAF bombers.
- 8. US 1st and 9th Armies begins offensive near Aachen.
- 25. V-2 kills 160 in London.

- 1. US 3rd Army reaches river Saar.
- 10. Free Norwegian forces destroy rail links to prevent evacuation of German troops from Norway to Germany.
- 16. Battle of the Bulge. Surprise German attack in the Ardennes smashes US defences and drives west towards Allied supply lines.
- 21. Germans reach Bastogne, but cannot overcome determined US resistance.
- 25. Germans halted at Celles.
- Allies lost 205 merchant ships in 1944.

EASTERN FRONT

- 24. US launch first B29 Superfortress bombing raid on Tokyo. Aircraft take off from India and refuel in China. It is decided this is not a viable long-term option. Future raids will be flown from Saipan and Tinian.
- 27. US warships off Philippines attacked by Japanese aircraft, several of which are reported to deliberately crash into the ships. These are the first attacks by Japanese kamikaze pilots.

- 7. US troops land at Ormoc, Philippines.
- 8. US warships bombard Japanese positions on the strategic island of Iwo Jima.
- 13. US B29 bombers from Saipan seriously damage Mitsubishi works at Nagoya, Japan.
- 15. US troops land on Mindoro, Philippines.
- 16. Chinese capture Bhamo.

THE MED AND MIDDLE EAST

- 29. Russian forces link up with Yugoslav Communist Resistance fighters at Pecs.

- 22. Russians set up puppet Communist government in occupied Hungary.
- 24. Russians reach Budapest and lay siege to powerful German forces in the city.

REST OF THE WORLD

- 4. Liberation of Greece completed.
- 25. British 8th Army crosses the river Cosina.

- 3. British troops break up battle between Greek royalists and Communists in Athens.
- 5. Greek Communists attack British troops. Greek civil war begins.

1945

World War II looks set to continue into 1946, but comes to an unexpectedly early end as the atomic bombs are unleashed.

RUSSIANS CAPTURE WARSAW

2. Heavy Allied bombing raids strike transport links behind German lines.

8. Allied armies clear German forces from west bank of the Maas.

15. German E-boats launch attack on Allied merchant ships in the Thames estuary.

16. German armies driven back to their position before the Battle of the Bulge.

6. 18 US warships, including two battleships, are badly damaged by kamikaze attacks.

9. Americans land at Lingayen, Philippines.

19. US launch heavy B29 raid on aircraft works at Kobe, Japan.

24. British Pacific Fleet attacks Japanese positions in Dutch East Indies.

25. Japanese begin evacuation of inland China.

12. Russians launch major offensive over the Vistula, advancing 40 km on first day.

17. Russians capture ruins of Warsaw.

23. Russians reach river Oder.

US MARINES LAND ON PACIFIC ISLAND OF IWO JIMA

▼ The Stars and Stripes flag is raised on Mount Suribachi, 23 February 1945.

3. Free French liberate Colmar.

3. 1000 US bombers strike Berlin in daylight, destroying airport and rail yards.

9. Ecuador, Peru and Paraguay declare war on Germany.

13. The Dresden Raid. 1000 British and American bombers obliterate Dresden to destroy transport links. Many German refugees are killed in the resulting firestorm.

22. Saudi Arabia, Turkey and Uruguay declare war on Germany and Japan.

16. US paratroops capture fortified island of Corregidor, Philippines.

19. US Marines land on Iwo Jima in the face of determined and skilful Japanese resistance.

23. US Marines take Mount Suribachi on Iwo Jima. Flag raising becomes the most famous photo of the war.

4. Yalta Conference. Churchill, Stalin and Roosevelt discuss post-war face of Europe.

4. Russians begin offensive over the Oder.

13. Russians capture Budapest.

KEY 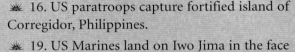 DIPLOMACY ⚓ HOME ⚓ NAVAL ⚓ SECRET WAR ⚔ BATTLE

GERMAN DEFENCES CRUMBLE ACROSS EUROPE

WESTERN FRONT

☀ 3. US 1st Army reaches Cologne.

☀ 7. US 1st Army captures bridge over the river Rhine at Remagen. Tanks and troops pour across to establish a bridgehead.

☀ 11. Precision raid by British bombers halts production at Krupps steel works, Essen.

☀ 17. Bridge at Remagen destroyed by attack by German Ar234 jet bombers. Americans have already built replacement pontoon bridges and continue to cross the river Rhine.

☀ 22. US 3rd Army crosses the river Rhine at Mainz using hurriedly assembled boats.

☀ 23. Operation Plunder. British cross the river Rhine at Wesel in strength. German resistance is at first slight, but soon stiffens.

☀ 25. British bombers destroy vast German oil reserves at Hamburg.

☀ 29. British armoured forces break out of Wesel bridgehead.

☀ 29. US 7th Army capture Heidelberg.

EASTERN FRONT

☀ 3. Americans capture Manila, Philippines.

☀ 8. British enter Mandalay, Burma.

☀ 9. US B29 bombers from Tinian and Guam launch firestorm raid on Tokyo that kills 84,000 and destroys 26 sq km of the city.

☀ 9. In Indo-China, the Japanese arrest or murder French officials and declare a puppet government.

☀ 16. Japanese counter attack at Meiktila, Burma, is defeated.

☀ 20. British capture Mandalay, Burma, and begin drive south towards Rangoon.

♠ 25. US naval forces arrive off Okinawa to begin preliminary bombardment and reconnaissance prior to landings.

☀ 26. US forces declare Iwo Jima 'secure', although isolated Japanese continue guerrilla actions for some days to come.

THE MED AND MIDDLE EAST

⌂ 8. Marshal Tito forms provisional Communist government in Yugoslavia.

☀ 11. Russians capture Küstrin and Tczew.

☀ 12. Russians capture Zvolen.

☀ 18. Poles capture Kolberg.

⌂ 19. Hitler orders his army to employ 'scorched earth' policy as they retreat.

☀ 22. Russians break German defences at Oppeln, Silesia.

REST OF THE WORLD

KEY   🤝 DIPLOMACY   ⌂ HOME   ♠ NAVAL   ⚓ SECRET WAR   ☀ BATTLE

US TROOPS INVADE JAPANESE ISLAND OF OKINAWA

⚜ 1. German Army Group B surrounded in Ruhr Valley by US and British armies.

⚜ 8. Americans capture Schweinfurt and Essen. Free French capture Pfrozheim.

⚜ 11. Americans reach river Elbe.

⚜ 13. Americans capture Jena.

⚜ 13. Americans capture Nuremburg.

⚜ 18. Canadians reach the Zuider Zee, Netherlands.

⚜ 19. German Army Group B – 400,000 men – surrenders in the Ruhr.

⚜ 25. British bombers attack Hitler's mountain retreat of Berchtesgarten in case he is seeking refuge there.

⚜ 26. Russian and US forces meet at Torgau on the river Elbe.

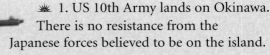

⚜ 1. US 10th Army lands on Okinawa. There is no resistance from the Japanese forces believed to be on the island.

⚜ 5. US forces on Okinawa meet first Japanese resistance from prepared defences.

⚜ 6. Massed kamikaze attacks on US fleet off Okinawa inflict heavy damage.

⚜ 14. Americans launch first attack on Japanese defences on Motobu Peninsula, Okinawa.

⚜ 23. Japanese on Okinawa withdraw to defensive positions around Shuri.

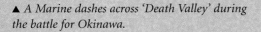

▲ *A Marine dashes across 'Death Valley' during the battle for Okinawa.*

⚜ 3. Russians capture Bratislava.

⚜ 6. Russians attack Vienna and Königsberg.

⚜ 13. Russians capture Vienna.

⚜ 16. Russians begin offensive on Berlin.

⚜ 21. Russians enter Berlin suburbs.

⚜ 24. Russians surround central Berlin.

⚱ 30. Hitler and other leading Nazis commit suicide at command bunker in Berlin.

⚜ 8. British 8th Army crosses river Senior.

⚜ 21. Allies capture Bologna.

⚜ 22. Allies reach banks of the river Po.

⚜ 25. Germans evacuate Genoa.

⚱ 28. Former Italian dictator Mussolini captured and shot by Communist partisans.

⚜ 29. One million Germans in Italy surrender.

GERMANY SURRENDERS   OKINAWA CAPTURED

WESTERN FRONT

♦ 1. German radio announces that Hitler is dead. Admiral Dönitz succeeds him as Führer of Germany.

� 4. All German forces on the Western Front surrender to British General Montgomery.

⚔ 4. Unconditional surrender of Germany signed by Field Marshal Jodl at Rheims.

♦ 8. VE (Victory in Europe) Day. Extensive celebrations throughout Allied countries.

⚔ 8. German forces in Norway surrender to recently returned Crown Prince Olaf.

🤝 3. Allies agree on boundaries of British, French, US and Russian zones of occupation in Germany.

EASTERN FRONT

⚔ 2. American attack on Shuri, Okinawa, is driven back with heavy loss.

⚔ 3. British–Indian army captures Rangoon.

⚔ 5. Japanese counter attack at Shuri, Okinawa, is defeated.

⚔ 10. Americans cross river Asa, Okinawa.

⚔ 14. Americans launch firestorm raid on Nagoya, Japan, destroying 36 sq km of city.

⚔ 21. Japanese withdraw from Shuri, Okinawa. Heavy rain halts US attacks.

⚔ 3. Japanese defenders on Okinawa now restricted to Oroku Peninsula.

🤝 6. Brazil declares war on Japan.

⚔ 10. American 24th Corps launches attack on remaining Japanese positions on Okinawa.

⚔ 22. Americans declare Okinawa to be secure.

THE MED AND MIDDLE EAST

⚔ 2. Russians capture Berlin.

⚔ 7. Siege of Breslau ends after 82 days.

⚔ 8. Formal German surrender ratified in Berlin by German Field Marshal Keitel and Russian Marshal Zhukov.

REST OF THE WORLD

KEY   🤝 DIPLOMACY   ♦ HOME   ⚓ NAVAL   🗡 SECRET WAR   ⚔ BATTLE

PHILIPPINES LIBERATED   JAPAN SURRENDERS

◄ *US General Douglas MacArthur signs the official end of the war onboard the battleship USS* Missouri *in Tokyo Bay.*

WESTERN FRONT

⬥ 4. US General MacArthur announces final liberation of the Philippines.

☀ 10. Raid by over 1000 B29 bombers pounds Tokyo area without loss.

🤝 12. Japanese Prince Konoye in Russia asks Stalin to pass on request to USA and Britain for peace terms. Stalin refuses.

⚓ 16. First atomic bomb tested at Alamogordo, New Mexico, USA.

☀ 24. Most of Japanese fleet sunk at Kure.

☀ 6. Hiroshima hit by first atomic bomb to be used in action. About 80,000 die instantly as 12 sq km of the city is destroyed.

☀ 9. Nagasaki hit by atomic bomb. About 40,000 die as 4 sq km of the city is destroyed.

🤝 14. Japan surrenders. The formal surrender document is signed on board USS *Missouri* in Tokyo Bay on 2 September.

▼ *Survivors wander through an unrecognizable landscape of bombed Nagasaki.*

EASTERN FRONT

THE MED AND MIDDLE EAST

REST OF THE WORLD